The Scientific Basis of Morals

Right and Wrong

The Ethics of Belief

The Ethics of Religion

William Kingdon Clifford, FRS

Solis Press

Originally published in 1884 as *The Scientific Basis of Morals, and Other Essays*, this edition republished in 2017 by Solis Press with additional notes (indicated by the use of square brackets) by George Cavendish.

This edition with annotations published 2017 by Solis Press.

Published by Solis Press, 2017
Annotations © 2017 George Cavendish
Typographical arrangement copyright © Solis Press 2017

ISBN: 978-1-910146-31-6

Published by Solis Press, PO Box 482,
Tunbridge Wells TN2 9QT, Kent, England

Web: www.solispress.com | *Twitter*: @SolisPress

Contents

1. The Scientific Basis of Morals

BY MORALS OR ETHIC I mean the doctrine of a special kind of pleasure or displeasure which is felt by the human mind in contemplating certain courses of conduct, whereby they are felt to be *right* or *wrong*, and of a special desire to do the right things and avoid the wrong ones. The pleasure or displeasure is commonly called the moral sense; the corresponding desire might be called the moral appetite. These are facts, existing in the consciousness of every man who need be considered in this discussion, and sufficiently marked out by these names; they need no further definition. In the same way the sense of taste is a feeling of pleasure or displeasure in things savoury or unsavoury, and is associated with a desire for the one and a repulsion from the other. We must assume that everybody knows what these words mean; the feelings they describe may be analysed or accounted for, but they cannot be more exactly defined as feelings.

The maxims of ethic are recommendations or commands of the form, 'Do this particular thing because it is right,' or 'Avoid this particular thing because it is wrong.' They express the immediate desire to do the right thing for itself, not for the sake of anything else: on this account the mood of them is called the categorical imperative. The particular things commanded or forbidden by such maxims depend upon the character of the individual in whose mind they arise. There is a certain general agreement in the ethical code of persons belonging to the same race at a given time, but considerable variations in different races and times. To the question 'What is right?' can therefore only be answered in the first instance, 'That which pleases your moral sense.' But it may be further asked 'What is generally thought right?' and the reply will specify the ethic of a particular race and period. But the ethical code of an individual, like the standard of taste, may be modified by habit and education; and accordingly the question may be asked, 'How shall I order my moral desires so as to be able to satisfy them most completely and continuously? What *ought* I to feel to be right?' The answer to this question must be sought in the study of the conditions under which the moral sense was produced and is preserved; in other words, in the study of its functions as a property of the human organism. The maxims derived from this study may be called maxims of abstract or absolute right; they are not absolutely universal, 'eternal and immutable,' but they are independent of the individual, and practically universal for the present condition of the human species.

I mean by Science the application of experience to new circumstances, by the aid of an order of nature which has been observed in the past, and on the assumption that such order will continue in the future. The simplest use of experience as a guide to action is probably not even conscious; it is the association by continually repeated selection of certain actions with certain circumstances, as in the unconsciously acquired craft of the maker of flint implements. I still call this science, although it is only a beginning; because the physiological process is a type of what takes place in all later stages. The next step may be expressed in the form of a hypothetical maxim—'If you want to make brass, melt your copper along with this blue stone.' To a maxim of this sort it may always be replied, 'I do not want to make brass, and so I shall not do as you tell me.' This reply is anticipated in the final form of science, when it is expressed as a statement or proposition: brass is an alloy of copper and zinc, and calamine[1] is zinc carbonate. Belief in a general statement is an artifice of our mental constitution, whereby infinitely various sensations and groups of sensations are brought into connection with infinitely various actions and groups of actions. On the phenomenal side there corresponds a certain cerebral structure by which various combinations of disturbances in the sensor tract are made to lead to the appropriate combinations of disturbances in the motor tract. The important point is that science, though apparently transformed into pure knowledge, has yet never lost its character of being a *craft*; and that it is not the knowledge itself which can rightly be called science, but a special way of getting and of using knowledge. Namely, science is the getting of knowledge from experience on the assumption of uniformity in nature, and the use of such knowledge to guide the actions of men. And the most abstract statements or propositions in science are to be regarded as bundles of hypothetical maxims packed into a portable shape and size. Every scientific fact is a shorthand expression for a vast number of practical directions: if you want so-and-so, do so-and-so.

If with this meaning of the word 'Science,' there is such a thing as a scientific basis of Morals, it must be true that:

---

1 [Calamine is an old-fashioned term referring to ores of zinc. There are two minerals: zinc carbonate and zinc silicate. *Calamine lotion* contains the pink mixture of zinc oxide and iron oxide.]

1. the maxims of Ethic are hypothetical maxims
2. derived from experience
3. on the assumption of uniformity in nature.

These propositions I shall now endeavour to prove; and in conclusion, I shall indicate the direction in which we may look for those general statements of fact whose organization will complete the likeness of ethical and physical science.

The Tribal Self

In the metaphysical sense, the word 'self' is taken to mean the conscious subject, *das Ich*,[2] the whole stream of feelings which make up a consciousness regarded as bound together by association and memory. But, in the more common and more restricted ethical sense, what we call *self* is a selected aggregate of feelings and of objects related to them, which hangs together as a conception by virtue of long and repeated association. My self does not include all my feelings, because habitually separate off some of them, say they do not properly belong to me, and treat them as my enemies. On the other hand, it does in general include my body regarded as an object, because of the feelings which occur simultaneously with events which affect it. My foot is certainly part of myself, because I get hurt when anybody treads on it. When we desire anything for its somewhat remote consequences, it is not common for these to be represented to the mind in the form of the actual feelings of pleasure which are ultimately to flow from the satisfaction of the desire; instead of this, they are replaced by a symbolic conception which represents the thing desired as doing good to the complex abstraction *self*. This abstraction serves thus to support and hold together those complex and remote motives which make up by far the greater part of the life of the intelligent races. When a thing is desired for no immediate pleasure that it can bring, it is generally desired on account of a certain symbolic substitute for pleasure, the feeling that this thing is suitable to the self. And, as in many like cases, this feeling, which at first derived its pleasurable nature from the faintly represented simple pleasures of which it was a symbol, ceases after a time to recall them and becomes a simple pleasure itself. In this way the self becomes a sort of centre about which our remoter motives revolve, and to which they always

---

2 ['The I' was considered by Sigmund Freud and when translated into English became the Latinized *ego*.]

W. K. CLIFFORD

have regard; in virtue of which, moreover, they become immediate and simple, from having been complex and remote.

If we consider now the simpler races of mankind, we shall find not only that immediate desires play a far larger part in their lives, and so that the conception of self is less used and less developed, but also that it is less definite and more wide. The savage is not only hurt when anybody treads on his foot, but when anybody treads on his tribe. He may lose his hut, and his wife, and his opportunities of getting food. In this way the tribe becomes naturally included in that conception of self which renders remote desires possible by making them immediate. The actual pains or pleasures which come from the woe or weal of the tribe, and which were the source of this conception, drop out of consciousness and are remembered no more; the symbol which has replaced them becomes a centre and goal of immediate desires, powerful enough in many cases to override the strongest suggestions of individual pleasure or pain.

Here a helping cause comes in. The tribe, *qua*[3] tribe, has to exist, and it can only exist by aid of such an organic artifice as the conception of the tribal self in the minds of its members. Hence the natural selection of those races in which this conception is the most powerful and most habitually predominant as a motive over immediate desires. To such an extent has this proceeded that we may fairly doubt whether the selfhood of the tribe is not earlier in point of development than that of the individual. In the process of time it becomes a matter of hereditary transmission, and is thus fixed as a specific character in the constitution of social man. With the settlement of countries, and the aggregation of tribes into nations, it takes a wider and more abstract form; and in the highest natures the tribal self is incarnate in nothing less than humanity. Short of these heights, it places itself in the family and in the city. I shall call that quality or disposition of man which consists in the supremacy of the family or tribal self as a mark of reference for motives by its old name *Piety*. And I have now to consider certain feelings and conceptions to which the existence of piety must necessarily give rise.

Before going further, however, it will be advisable to fix as precisely as may be the sense of the words just used. Self, then, in the ethical sense, is a conception in the mind of the individual which serves as a peg on which remote desires are hung and by which they are rendered immediate. The individual self is such a peg for the hanging of remote

---

3 [In the capacity of; or as being.]

8

desires which affect the individual only. The tribal self is a conception in the mind of the individual which serves as a peg on which those remote desires are hung which were implanted in him by the need of the tribe as a tribe. We must carefully distinguish the tribal self from society, or the 'common consciousness'; it is something in the mind of each individual man which binds together his gregarious instincts.

The word *tribe* is here used to mean a group of that size which in the circumstances considered is selected for survival or destruction *as a group*. Self-regarding excellences are brought out by the natural selection of individuals; the tribal self is developed by the natural selection of groups. The size of the groups must vary at different times; and the extent of the tribal self must vary accordingly.

Approbation and Conscience

The tribe has to exist. Such tribes as saw no necessity for it have ceased to live. To exist, it must encourage piety; and there is a method which lies ready to hand.

We do not like a man whose character is such that we may reasonably expect injuries from him. This dislike of a man on account of his character is a more complex feeling than the mere dislike of separate injuries. A cat likes your hand and your lap, and the food you give her; but I do not think she has any conception of *you*. A dog, however, may like *you* even when you thrash him, though he does not like the thrashing. Now such likes and dislikes may be felt by the tribal self. If a man does anything generally regarded as good for the tribe, my tribal self may say, in the first place, 'I like that thing that you have done.' By such common approbation of individual acts the influence of piety as a motive becomes defined; and natural selection will in the long run preserve those tribes which have approved the right things; namely, those things which at that time gave the tribe an advantage in the struggle for existence. But in the second place, a man may as a rule and constantly, being actuated by piety, do good things for the tribe; and in that case the tribal self will say, I like *you*. The feeling expressed by this statement on the part of any individual, 'In the name of the tribe, I like you,' is what I call *approbation*. It is the feeling produced in pious individuals by that sort of character which seems to them beneficial to the community.

Now suppose that a man has done something obviously harmful to the community. Either some immediate desire, or his individual self, has for once proved stronger than the tribal self. When the tribal self wakes up, the man says, 'In the name of the tribe, I do not like this thing that I, as an individual, have done.' This Self-judgement in the name of the tribe is called Conscience. If the man goes further and draws from this act and others an inference about his own character, he may say, 'In the name of the tribe, I do not like my individual self.' This is remorse. Mr. Darwin has well pointed out that immediate desires are in general strong but of short duration,[4] and cannot be adequately represented to the mind after they have passed; while the social forces, though less violent, have a steady and continuous action.

In a mind sufficiently developed to distinguish the individual from the tribal self, conscience is thus a necessary result of the existence of piety; it is ready to hand as a means for its increase. But to account for the existence of piety and conscience in the elemental form which we have hitherto considered is by no means to account for the present moral nature of man. We shall be led many steps in that direction if we consider the way in which society has used these feelings of the individual as a means for its own preservation.

Right and Responsibility

A like or a dislike is one thing; the expression of it is another. It is attached to the feeling by links of association; and when this association has been selectively modified by experience, whether consciously or unconsciously, the expression serves a *purpose* of retaining or repeating the thing liked, and of removing the thing disliked. Such a purpose is served by the expression of tribal approbation or disapprobation, however little it may be the conscious end of such expression to any individual. It is necessary to the tribe that the pious character should be encouraged and preserved, the impious character discouraged and removed. The process is of two kinds; direct and reflex. In the direct process the tribal dislike of the offender is precisely similar to the dislike of a noxious beast; and it expresses itself in his speedy removal. But in the reflex process we find the first trace of that singular and wonderful judgement by analogy which ascribes to other men a consciousness similar to our own. If the process were a conscious one, it might perhaps be described in this way: the tribal self says, 'Put yourself in this man's place; he also is pious, but he has offended, and

---

4 [Charles Darwin, 1871, *The Descent of Man and Selection in Relation to Sex*: 'It is clear that many instinctive desires, such as that of hunger, are in their nature of short duration; and after being satisfied, are not readily or vividly recalled.']

that proves that he is not pious enough. Still, he has some conscience, and the expression of your tribal dislike to his character, awakening his conscience, will tend to change him and make him more pious.' But the process is not a conscious one: the social craft or art of living together is learned by the tribe and not by the individual, and the purpose of improving men's characters is provided for by complex social arrangements long before it has been conceived by any conscious mind. The tribal self learns to approve certain expressions of tribal liking or disliking; the actions whose open approval is liked by the tribal self are called right actions, and those whose open disapproval is liked are called wrong actions. The corresponding characters are called good or bad, virtuous or vicious.

This introduces a further complication into the conscience. Self-judgement in the name of the tribe becomes associated with very definite and material judgement by the tribe itself. On the one hand, this undoubtedly strengthens the motive-power of conscience in an enormous degree. On the other hand, it tends to guide the decisions of conscience; and since the expression of public approval or disapproval is made in general by means of some organized machinery of government, it becomes possible for conscience to be knowingly directed by the wise or misdirected by the wicked, instead of being driven along the right path by the slow selective process of experience. Now right actions are not those which are publicly approved, but those whose public approbation a well-instructed tribal self would like. Still, it is impossible to avoid the guiding influence of expressed approbation on the great mass of the people; and in those cases where the machinery of government is approximately a means of expressing the true public conscience, that influence becomes a most powerful help to improvement.

Let us note now the very important difference between the direct and the reflex process. To clear a man away as a noxious beast, and to punish him for doing wrong, these are two very different things. The purpose in the first case is merely to get rid of a nuisance; the purpose in the second case is to improve the character either of the man himself or of those who will observe this public expression of disapprobation. The offence of which the man has been guilty leads to an inference about his character, and it is supposed that the community may contain other persons whose characters are similar to his, or tend to become so. It has been found that the expression of public disapprobation tends to awake the conscience of such people and to improve their characters. If the improvement of the man himself is aimed at, it is assumed that he has a conscience which can be worked upon and made to deter him from similar offences in future.

The word *purpose* has here been used in a sense to which it is perhaps worthwhile to call attention. Adaptation of means to an end may be produced in two ways that we at present know of; by processes of natural selection, and by the agency of an intelligence in which an image or idea of the end preceded the use of the means. In both cases the existence of the adaptation is accounted for by the necessity or utility of the end. It seems to me convenient to use the word *purpose* as meaning generally the end to which certain means are adapted, both in these two cases, and in any other that may hereafter become known, provided only that the adaptation is accounted for by the necessity or utility of the end. And there seems no objection to the use of the phrase 'final cause' in this wider sense, if it is to be kept at all. The word 'design' might then be kept for the special case of adaptation by an intelligence. And we may then say that since the process of natural selection has been understood, *purpose* has ceased to suggest *design* to instructed people, except in cases where the agency of man is independently probable.

When a man can be punished for doing wrong with approval of the tribal self, he is said to be *responsible*. Responsibility implies two things:—(1) The act was a product of the man's character and of the circumstances, and his character may to a certain extent be inferred from the act; (2) The man had a conscience which might have been so worked upon as to prevent his doing the act. Unless the first condition be fulfilled, we cannot reasonably take any action at all in regard to the man, but only in regard to the offence. In the case of crimes of violence, for example, we might carry a six-shooter to protect ourselves against similar possibilities, but unless the fact of a man's having once committed a murder made it probable that he would do the like again, it would clearly be absurd and unreasonable to lynch the man. That is to say, we assume a uniformity of connection between character and actions, infer a man's character from his past actions, and endeavour to provide against his future actions either by destroying him or by changing his character. I think it will be found that in all those cases where we not only deal with the offence but treat it with moral reprobation, we imply the existence of a conscience which might have been worked upon to improve the character. Why, for example, do we not regard a lunatic as responsible? Because we are in possession of information about his character derived not only from his one offence but from other facts, whereby we know that even if he had a conscience left, his mind is so diseased that it is impossible by moral reprobation alone to change his character so that it may be subsequently relied upon. With his cure from disease and the restored validity of this condition, responsibility returns. There are, of course, cases in which an irresponsible person is punished as if he were responsible, *pour encourager les autres*[5] who are responsible. The question of the right or wrong of this procedure is the question of its average effect on the character of men at any particular time.

The Categorical Imperative

May we now say that the maxims of Ethic are hypothetical maxims? I think we may, and that in showing why we shall explain the apparent difference between them and other maxims belonging to an early stage of science. In the first place ethical maxims are learned by the tribe and not by the individual. Those tribes have on the whole survived in which conscience approved such actions as tended to the improvement of men's characters as citizens and therefore to the survival of the tribe. Hence it is that the moral sense of the individual, though founded on the experience of the tribe, is purely intuitive; conscience gives no reasons. Notwithstanding this, the ethical maxims are presented to us as conditional; if you want to live together in this complicated way, your ways must be straight and not crooked, you must seek the truth and love no lie. Suppose we answer, 'I don't want to live together with other men in this complicated way; and so I shall not do as you tell me.' That is not the end of the matter, as it might be with other scientific precepts. For obvious reasons it is *right* in this case to reply, 'Then in the name of my people I do not like you,' and to express this dislike by appropriate methods. And the offender, being descended from a social race, is unable to escape his conscience, the voice of his tribal self which says, 'In the name of the tribe, I hate myself for this treason that I have done.'

There are two reasons, then, why ethical maxims appear to be unconditional. First, they are acquired from experience not directly but by tribal selection, and therefore in the mind of the individual they do not rest upon the true reasons for them. Secondly, although they are

---

5 ['To encourage the others.' The phrase is thought to have come from Voltaire's *Candide*, 1759, when referring to the execution of a British admiral for his failings: '*Dans ce pays-ci, il est bon de tuer de temps en temps un amiral pour encourager les autres.*' 'In this country, it is wise to kill an admiral from time to time to encourage the others.']

conditional, the absence of the condition in one born of a social race is rightly visited by moral reprobation.

Ethics are based on Uniformity

I have already observed that to deal with men as a means of influencing their actions implies that these actions are a product of character and circumstances; and that moral reprobation and responsibility cannot exist unless we assume the efficacy of certain special means of influencing character. It is not necessary to point out that such considerations involve that uniformity of nature which underlies the possibility of even unconscious adaptations to experience, of language, and of general conceptions and statements. It may be asked, 'Are you quite sure that these observed uniformities between motive and action, between character and motive, between social influence and change of character, are absolutely exact in the form in which you state them, or indeed that they are exact laws of any form? May there not be very slight divergences from exact laws, which will allow of the action of an "uncaused will," or of the interference of some "extra-mundane force"?' I am sure I do not know. But this I do know: that our sense of right and wrong is derived from such order as we can observe, and not from such caprice of disorder as we may fancifully conjecture; and that to whatever extent a divergence from exactness became sensible, to that extent it would destroy the most widespread and worthy of the acquisitions of mankind.

The Final Standard

By these views we are led to conclusions partly negative, partly positive; of which, as might be expected, the negative are the most definite.

First, then, Ethic is a matter of the tribe or community, and therefore there are no 'self-regarding virtues.' The qualities of courage, prudence, etc., can only be *rightly* encouraged in so far as they are shown to conduce to the efficiency of a citizen; that is, in so far as they cease to be self-regarding. The duty of private judgement, of searching after truth, the sacredness of belief which ought not to be misused on unproved statements, follow only on showing of the enormous importance to society of a true knowledge of things. And any diversion of conscience from its sole allegiance to the community is condemned *a priori* in the very nature of right and wrong.

Next, the end of Ethic is not the greatest happiness of the greatest number. Your happiness is of no use to the community, except in so far as it tends to make you a more efficient citizen—that is to say, happiness is not to be desired for its own sake, but for the sake of something else. If any end is pointed to, it is the end of increased efficiency in each man's special work, as well as in the social functions which are common to all. A man must strive to be a better citizen, a better workman, a better son, husband, or father.

Again, Piety is not Altruism. It is not the doing good to others as others, but the service of the community by a member of it, who loses in that service the consciousness that he is anything different from the community.

The social organism, like the individual, may be healthy or diseased. Health and disease are very difficult things to define accurately: but for practical purposes, there are certain states about which no mistake can be made. When we have even a very imperfect catalogue and description of states that are clearly and certainly diseases, we may form a rough preliminary definition of health by saying that it means the absence of all these states. Now the health of society involves among other things, that right is done by the individuals composing it. And certain social diseases consist in a wrong direction of the conscience. Hence the determination of abstract right depends on the study of healthy and diseased states of society. How much light can be got for this end from the historical records we possess? A very great deal, if, as I believe, for ethical purposes the nature of man and of society may be taken as approximately constant during the few thousand years of which we have distinct records.

The matters of fact on which rational ethic must be founded are the laws of modification of character, and the evidence of history as to those kinds of character which have most aided the improvement of the race. For although the moral sense is intuitive, it must for the future be directed by our conscious discovery of the tribal purpose which it serves.

2. Right and Wrong: The Scientific Ground of their Distinction[6]

THE QUESTIONS WHICH ARE here to be considered are especially and peculiarly everybody's questions. It is not everybody's business to be an engineer, or a doctor, or a carpenter, or a soldier; but it is everybody's business to be a citizen. The doctrines and precepts which guide the practice of the good engineer are of interest to him who uses them and to those whose business it is to investigate them by mechanical science; the rest of us neither obey nor disobey them. But the doctrines and precepts of morality, which guide the practice of the good citizen, are of interest to all; they must be either obeyed or disobeyed by every human being who is not hopelessly and forever separated from the rest of mankind. No one can say, therefore, that in this enquiry we are not minding our own business, that we are meddling with other men's affairs. We are in fact studying the principles of our profession, so far as we are able; a necessary thing for every man who wishes to do good work in it.

Along with the character of universal interest which belongs to our subject there goes another. What is everybody's practical business is also to a large extent what everybody knows; and it may be reasonably expected that a discourse about Right and Wrong will be full of platitudes and truisms. The expectation is a just one. The considerations I have to offer are of the very oldest and the very simplest commonplace and common sense; and no one can be more astonished than I am that there should be any reason to speak of them at all. But there is reason to speak of them, because platitudes are not all of one kind. Some platitudes have a definite meaning and a practical application, and are established by the uniform and long-continued experience of all people. Other platitudes, having no definite meaning and no practical application, seem not to be worth anybody's while to test; and these are quite sufficiently established by mere assertion, if it is audacious enough to begin with and persistent enough afterward. It is in order to distinguish these two kinds of platitude from one another, and to make

---

6 Sunday Lecture Society, 7 November 1875.

sure that those which we retain form a body of doctrine consistent with itself and with the rest of our beliefs, that we undertake this examination of obvious and widespread principles.

First of all, then, what are the facts?

We say that it is wrong to murder, to steal, to tell lies, and that it is right to take care of our families. When we say in this sense that one action is right and another wrong, we have a certain feeling toward the action which is peculiar and not quite like any other feeling. It is clearly a feeling toward the action and not toward the man who does it; because we speak of hating the sin and loving the sinner. We might reasonably dislike a man whom we knew or suspected to be a murderer, because of the natural fear that he might murder us; and we might like our own parents for taking care of us. But everybody knows that these feelings are something quite different from the feeling which condemns murder as a wrong thing, and approves parental care as a right thing. I say nothing here about the possibility of analysing this feeling, or proving that it arises by combination of other feelings; all I want to notice is that it is as distinct and recognizable as the feeling of pleasure in a sweet taste or of displeasure at a toothache. In speaking of right and wrong, we speak of qualities of action which arouse definite feelings that everybody knows and recognizes. It is not necessary, then, to give a definition at the outset; we are going to use familiar terms which have a definite meaning in the same sense in which everybody uses them. We may ultimately come to something like a definition; but what we have to do first is to collect the facts and see what can be made of them, just as if we were going to talk about limestone, or parents and children, or fuel.

It is easy to conceive that murder and theft and neglect of the young might be considered wrong in a very simple state of society. But we find at present that the condemnation of these actions does not stand alone; it goes with the condemnation of a great number of other actions which seem to be included with the obviously criminal action, in a sort of general rule. The wrongness of murder, for example, belongs in a less degree to any form of bodily injury that one man may inflict on another; and it is even extended so as to include injuries to his reputation or his feelings. I make these more refined precepts follow in the train of the more obvious and rough ones, because this appears to have been the traditional order of their establishment. 'He that makes his neighbour blush in public,' says the Mishnah, 'is as if he had shed his blood.[7] In the same way the rough condemnation of stealing carries with it a condemnation of more refined forms of dishonesty: we do not hesitate to say that it is wrong for a tradesman to adulterate his goods, or for a labourer to scamp his work. We not only say that it is wrong to tell lies, but that it is wrong to deceive in other more ingenious ways; wrong to use words so that they shall have one sense to some people and another sense to other people; wrong to suppress the truth when that suppression leads to false belief in others. And again, the duty of parents toward their children is seen to be a special case of a very large and varied class of duties toward that great family to which we belong—to the fatherland and them that dwell therein. The word *duty* which I have here used, has as definite a sense to the general mind as the words *right* and *wrong*; we say that it is right to do our duty, and wrong to neglect it. These duties to the community serve in our minds to explain and define our duties to individuals. It is wrong to kill anyone; unless we are an executioner, when it may be our duty to kill a criminal; or a soldier, when it may be our duty to kill the enemy of our country; and in general it is wrong to injure any man in any way in our private capacity and for our own sakes. Thus if a man injures us, it is only right to retaliate on behalf of other men. Of two men in a desert island, if one takes away the other's cloak, it may or may not be right for the other to let him have his coat also; but if a man takes away my cloak while we both live in society, it is my duty to use such means as I can to prevent him from taking away other people's cloaks. Observe that I am endeavouring to describe the facts of the moral feelings of Englishmen, such as they are now.

The last remark leads us to another platitude of exceedingly ancient date. We said that it was wrong to injure any man in our private capacity and for our own sakes. A rule like this differs from all the others that we have considered, because it not only deals with physical acts, words and deeds which can be observed and known by others, but also with thoughts which are known only to the man himself. Who can tell whether a given act of punishment was done from a private or from a public motive? Only the agent himself. And yet if the punishment was just and within the law, we should condemn the man in the one case and approve him in the other. This pursuit of the actions of men

---

7 [There are various versions of this: 'He who insults a person in public is morally as guilty as if he had shed blood', *Bava Metzia* 58b. The Mishnah is part of the Jewish Torah.]

to their very sources, in the feelings which they only can know, is as ancient as any morality we know of, and extends to the whole range of it. Injury to another man arises from anger, malice, hatred, revenge; these feelings are condemned as wrong. But feelings are not immediately under our control, in the same way that overt actions are: I can shake anybody by the hand if I like, but I cannot always feel friendly to him. Nevertheless we can pay attention to such aspects of the circumstances, and we can put ourselves into such conditions, that our feelings get gradually modified in one way or the other; we form a habit of checking our anger by calling up certain images and considerations, whereby in time the offending passion is brought into subjection and control. Accordingly we say that it is right to acquire and to exercise this control; and the control is supposed to exist whenever we say that one feeling or disposition of mind is right and another wrong. Thus, in connection with the precept against stealing, we condemn envy and covetousness; we applaud a sensitive honesty which shudders at anything underhand or dishonourable. In connection with the rough precept against lying, we have built up and are still building a great fabric of intellectual morality, whereby a man is forbidden to tell lies to himself, and is commanded to practise candour and fairness and open-mindedness in his judgements, and to labour zealously in pursuit of the truth. In connection with the duty to our families, we say that it is right to cultivate public spirit, a quick sense of sympathy, and all that belongs to a social disposition.

Two other words are used in this connection which it seems necessary to mention. When we regard an action as right or wrong for ourselves, this feeling about the action impels us to do it or not to do it, as the case may be. We may say that the moral sense acts in this case as a motive; meaning by moral sense only the feeling in regard to an action which is considered as right or wrong, and by motive something which impels us to act. Of course there may be other motives at work at the same time, and it does not at all follow that we shall do the right action or abstain from the wrong one. This we all know to our cost. But still our feeling about the rightness or wrongness of an action does operate as a motive when we think of the action as being done by us; and when so operating it is called *conscience*. I have nothing to do at present with the questions about conscience, whether it is a result of education, whether it can be explained by self-love, and so forth; I am only concerned in describing well-known facts, and in getting as clear as I can about the meaning of well-known words. Conscience, then, is the whole aggregate of our feelings about actions as being right or wrong, regarded as tending to make us do the right actions and avoid the wrong ones. We also say sometimes, in answer to the question, 'How do you know that this is right or wrong?' 'My conscience tells me so.' And this way of speaking is quite analogous to other expressions of the same form; thus if I put my hand into water, and you ask me how I know that it is hot, I might say, 'My feeling of warmth tells me so.'

When we consider a right or a wrong action as done by another person, we think of that person as worthy of moral approbation or reprobation. He may be punished or not; but in any case this feeling toward him is quite different from the feeling of dislike toward a person injurious to us, or of disappointment at a machine which will not go.

Whenever we can morally approve or disapprove a man for his action, we say that he is morally responsible for it, and *vice versa*. To say that a man is not morally responsible for his actions is the same thing as to say that it would be unreasonable to praise or blame him for them.

The statement that we ourselves are morally responsible is somewhat more complicated, but the meaning is very easily made out; namely, that another person may reasonably regard our actions as right or wrong, and may praise or blame us for them.

We can now, I suppose, understand one another pretty clearly in using the words right and wrong, conscience, responsibility; and we have made a rapid survey of the facts of the case in our own country at the present time. Of course I do not pretend that this survey in any way approaches to completeness; but it will supply us at least with enough facts to enable us to deal always with concrete examples instead of remaining in generalities; and it may serve to show pretty fairly what the moral sense of an Englishman is like. We must next consider what account we can give of these facts by the scientific method.

But first let us stop to note that we really have used the scientific method in making this first step; and also that to the same extent the method has been used by all serious moralists. Some would have us define virtue, to begin with, in terms of some other thing which is not virtue, and then work out from our definition all the details of what we ought to do. So Plato said that virtue was knowledge,[8] Aristotle that it

---

8 [Plato (BC 428–347) was a Ancient Greek philosopher and a follower of Socrates who stated that virtue is knowledge.]

was the golden mean,[9] and Bentham[10] said that the right action was that which conduced to the greatest happiness of the greatest number. But so also, in physical speculations, Thales said that everything was Water, and Heraclitus said it was All-becoming, and Empedocles said it was made out of Four Elements, and Pythagoras said it was Number. But we only began to know about things when people looked straight at the facts, and made what they could out of them; and that is the only way in which we can know anything about right and wrong. Moreover, it is the way in which the great moralists have set to work, when they came to treat of verifiable things and not of theories all in the air. A great many people think of a prophet as a man who, all by himself, or from some secret source, gets the belief that this thing is right and that thing wrong. And then (they imagine) he gets up and goes about persuading other people to feel as he does about it; and so it becomes a part of their conscience, and a new duty is created. This may be in some cases, but I have never met with any example of it in history. When Socrates puzzled the Greeks by asking them what they precisely meant by Goodness and Justice and Virtue, the mere existence of the words shows that the people, as a whole, possessed a moral sense, and felt that certain things were right and others wrong. What the moralist did was to show the connection between different virtues, the likeness of virtue to certain other things, the implications which a thoughtful man could find in the common language. Wherever the Greek moral sense had come from, it was there in the people before it could be enforced by a prophet or discussed by a philosopher. Again, we find a wonderful collection of moral aphorisms in those shrewd sayings of the Jewish fathers which are preserved in the Mishnah or oral law. Some of this teaching is familiar to us all from the popular exposition of it which is contained in the three first Gospels. But the very plainness and homeliness of the precepts shows that they are just acute statements of what was already felt by the popular common sense; protesting, in many cases, against the formalism of the ceremonial law with which they are curiously mixed up. The Rabbis even show a jealousy of prophetic interference, as if they knew well that it takes not one man, but many men, to feel what is right. When a certain Rabbi Eliezer, being

---

9 [The middle way; the path between two extremes.]

10 [Jeremy Bentham (1748–1832), an English philosopher. He said that the 'fundamental axiom' of his philosophy was the principle that 'it is the greatest happiness of the greatest number that is the measure of right and wrong'.]

worsted in argument, cried out, 'If I am right, let heaven pronounce in my favour!' there was heard a Bath-kol or voice from the skies, saying, 'Do you venture to dispute with Rabbi Eliezer, who is an authority on all religious questions?' But Rabbi Joshua rose and said, 'Our law is not in heaven, but in the book which dates from Sinai, and which teaches us that in matters of discussion the majority makes the law.'[11]

One of the most important expressions of the moral sense for all time is that of the Stoic philosophy, especially after its reception among the Romans. It is here that we find the enthusiasm of humanity—the *caritas generis humani*[12]—which is so large and important a feature in all modern conceptions of morality, and whose widespread influence upon Roman citizens may be traced in the Epistles of St. Paul. In the Stoic emperors, also, we find probably the earliest example of great moral principles consciously applied to legislation on a large scale. But are we to attribute this to the individual insight of the Stoic philosophers? It might seem at first sight that we must, if we are to listen to that vulgar vituperation of the older culture which has descended to us from those who had everything to gain by its destruction.[13] We hear

---

11 Treatise *Bava Bathra*, 59b.

12 [For the love of humankind.]

13 Compare these passages from [Charles] Merivale ([*History of the*] *Romans under the Empire*, vi, [1872]), to whom 'it seems a duty to protest against the common tendency of Christian moralists to dwell only on the dark side of Pagan society, in order to heighten by contrast the blessings of the Gospel':

> 'Much candour and discrimination are required in comparing the sins of one age with those of another ... the cruelty of our inquisitions and sectarian persecutions, of our laws against sorcery, our serfdom and our slavery; the petty fraudulence we tolerate in almost every class and calling of the community; the bold front worn by our open sensuality; the deeper degradation of that which is concealed; all these leave us little room for boasting of our modern discipline, and must deter the thoughtful enquirer from too confidently contrasting the morals of the old world and the new.'

> 'Even at Rome, in the worst of times ... all the relations of life were adorned in turn with bright instances of devotion, and mankind transacted their business with an ordinary confidence in the force of conscience and right reason. The steady development of enlightened legal principles conclusively proves the general dependence upon law as a guide and corrector of manners. In the camp, however, more especially, as the chief sphere of this purifying activity, the great qualities of the Roman character continued to be plainly manifested. This history of the Caesars presents to us a constant succession of brave, patient, resolute, and faithful

enough of the luxurious feasting of the Roman capital, how it would almost have taxed the resources of a modern pastry-cook; of the cruelty of gladiatorial shows, how they were nearly as bad as *autos-da-fé*,[14] except that a man had his fair chance and was not tortured for torture's sake; of the oppression of provincials by people like Verres,[15] of whom it may even be said that if they had been the East India Company[16] they could not have been worse; of the complaints of Tacitus[17] against bad and mad emperors (as Sir Henry Maine[18] says); and of the still more serious complaints of the modern historian against the excessive taxation[19] which was one great cause of the fall of the empire. Of all this we are told a great deal; but we are not told of the many thousands of honourable men who carried civilization to the ends of the known world, and administered a mighty empire so that it was loved and worshiped to the furthest corner of it. It is to these men and their common action that we must attribute the morality which found its organized expression in the writings of the Stoic philosophers. From these three cases we may gather that Right is a thing which must be done before it can be talked about, although after that it may only too easily be talked about without being done. Individual effort and energy may insist upon getting that done which was already felt to be right; and individual insight and acumen may point out consequences of an action which bring it under previously known moral rules. There is another dispute of the Rabbis that may serve to show what is meant by this. It was forbidden

---

soldiers, men deeply impressed with a sense of duty, superior to vanity, despisers of boasting, content to toil in obscurity and shed their blood at the frontiers of the empire, unrepining at the cold mistrust of their masters, not clamorous for the honours so sparingly awarded to them, but satisfied in the daily work of their hands, and full of faith in the national destiny which they were daily accomplishing.'

14 [The burning of heretics during the Spanish Inquisition.]

15 [Gius Verres (BC120–43) was the Roman governor of Sicily who abused his authority.]

16 [A British trading company that came to rule large areas of India.]

17 [A Roman senator who was a historian and examined the reigns of Tiberius, Claudius and Nero.]

18 [Henry James Sumner Maine (1822–88) was a Scottish historian.]

19 Finlay, *Greece under the Romans*. [George Finlay, *Greece under the Romans, A historical view of the condition of the Greek nation from its conquest by the Romans until the extinction of the Roman power in the East, B.C. CXLVI to A.D. DCCXVI*, 1857.]

by the law to have any dealings with the Sabian idolaters[20] during the week preceding their idolatrous feasts. But the doctors discussed the case in which one of these idolaters owes you a bill; are you to let him pay it during that week or not? The school of Shammai[21] said 'No; for he will want all his money to enjoy himself at the feast.' But the school of Hillel[22] said, 'Yes, let him pay it; for how can he enjoy his feast while his bills are unpaid?' The question here is about the consequences of an action; but there is no dispute about the moral principle, which is that consideration and kindness are to be shown to idolaters, even in the matter of their idolatrous rites.

It seems, then, that we are no worse off than anybody else who has studied this subject, in finding our materials ready made for us; sufficiently definite meanings given in the common speech to the words right and wrong, good and bad, with which we have to deal; a fair body of facts familiarly known, which we have to organize and account for as best we can. But our special enquiry is, what account can be given of these facts by the scientific method? to which end we cannot do better than fix our ideas as well as we can upon the character and scope of that method.

Now the scientific method is a method of getting knowledge by inference, and that of two different kinds. One kind of inference is that which is used in the physical and natural sciences, and it enables us to go from known phenomena to unknown phenomena. Because a stone is heavy in the morning, I infer that it will be heavy in the afternoon; and I infer this by assuming a certain uniformity of nature. The sort of uniformity that I assume depends upon the extent of my scientific education; the rules of inference become more and more definite as we go on. At first I might assume that all things are always alike; this would not be true, but it has to be assumed in a vague way, in order that a thing may have the same name at different times. Afterward I get

---

20 [Sabians are mentioned in the Quran as a religious group alongside Jews and Christians. They still exist as a sect in the Middle East and are described as neither Muslim nor Christian but followers of John the Baptist who worship stellar angels.]

21 [A school of thought of Judaism founded by Shammai, a Jewish scholar of the first century BC. Shammai was an important contributor to the Mishnah.]

22 [A school of Jewish law and thought founded by the Hillel the Elder which thrived in first-century BC Jerusalem. Like Shammai, Hillel was an important contributor to the Mishnah and is thought to have been the author of the Golden Rule: 'That which is hateful to you, do not do to your fellow.']

the more definite belief that certain particular qualities, like weight, have nothing to do with the time of day; and subsequently I find that weight has nothing to do with the shape of the stone, but only with the quantity of it. The uniformity which we assume, then, is not that vague one that we started with, but a chastened and corrected uniformity. I might go on to suppose, for example, that the weight of the stone had nothing to do with the place where it was; and a great deal might be said for this supposition. It would, however, have to be corrected when it was found that the weight varies slightly in different latitudes. On the other hand, I should find that this variation was just the same for my stone as for a piece of iron or wood; that it had nothing to do with the kind of matter. And so I might be led to the conclusion that all matter is heavy, and that the weight of it depends only on its quantity and its position relative to the earth. You see here that I go on arriving at conclusions always of this form; that some one circumstance or quality has nothing to do with some other circumstance or quality. I begin by assuming that it is independent of everything; I end by finding that it is independent of some definite things. That is, I begin by assuming a vague uniformity. I always use this assumption to infer from some one fact a great number of other facts; but as my education proceeds, I get to know what sort of things may be inferred and what may not. An observer of scientific mind takes note of just those things from which inferences may be drawn, and passes by the rest. If an astronomer, observing the sun, were to record the fact that at the moment when a sunspot began to shrink there was a rap at his front door, we should know that he was not up to his work. But if he records that sunspots are thickest every eleven years, and that this is also the period of extra cloudiness in Jupiter, the observation may or may not be confirmed, and it may or may not lead to inferences of importance; but still it is the kind of thing from which inferences may be drawn. There is always a certain instinct among instructed people which tells them in this way what kinds of inferences may be drawn; and this is the unconscious effect of the definite uniformity which they have been led to assume in nature. It may subsequently be organized into a law or general truth, and no doubt becomes a surer guide by that process. Then it goes to form the more precise instinct of the next generation.

What we have said about this first kind of inference, which goes from phenomena to phenomena, is shortly this. It proceeds upon an assumption of uniformity in nature; and this assumption is not fixed and made once for all, but is a changing and growing thing, becoming more definite as we go on.

If I were told to pick out some one character which especially colours this guiding conception of uniformity in our present stage of science, I should certainly reply, Atomism. The form of this with which we are most familiar is the molecular theory of bodies; which represents all bodies as made up of small elements of uniform character, each practically having relations only with the adjacent ones, and these relations the same all through—namely, some simple mechanical action upon each other's motions. But this is only a particular case. A palace, a cottage, the tunnel of the underground railway, and a factory chimney, are all built of bricks; the bricks are alike in all these cases, each brick is practically related only to the adjacent ones, and the relation is throughout the same, namely, two flat sides are stuck together with mortar. There is an atomism in the sciences of number, of quantity, of space; the theorems of geometry are groupings of individual points, each related only to the adjacent ones by certain definite laws. But what concerns us chiefly at present is the atomism of human physiology. Just as every solid is built up of molecules, so the nervous system is built up of nerve-threads and nerve-corpuscles. We owe to Mr. Lewes[23] our very best thanks for the stress which he has laid on the doctrine that nerve-fibre is uniform in structure and function, and for the word *neurility*,[24] which expresses its common properties. And similar gratitude is due to Dr. Hughlings Jackson[25] for his long defence of the proposition that the element of nervous structure and function is a sensorimotor[26] process. In structure, this is two fibres or bundles of fibres going to the same grey corpuscle; in function it is a message travelling up one fibre or bundle to the corpuscle, and then down the other fibre or bundle. Out of this, as a brick, the house of our life is built. All these simple elementary processes are alike, and each is practically related only to the adjacent ones; the relation being in all cases of the same kind, viz., the passage from a simple to a complex message, or *vice versa*.

The result of atomism in any form, dealing with any subject, is that the principle of uniformity is hunted down into the elements of things;

---

23 [George Henry Lewes (1817–78) was an English philosopher and literarist. As well as his literary pursuits he developed an interest in biology. He lived with Mary Ann Evans, better know by her *nom de plume* of George Eliot.]

24 [A term no longer used relating to the properties of nerve tissue.]

25 [John Hughlings Jackson (1835–1911) was an English neurologist specializing in epilepsy.]

26 [Having both sensory and motor functions.]

it is resolved into the uniformity of these elements or atoms, and of the relations of those which are next to each other. By an element or an atom we do not here mean something absolutely simple or indivisible, for a molecule, a brick, and a nerve-process are all very complex things. We only mean that, for the purpose in hand, the properties of the still more complex thing which is made of them have nothing to do with the complexities or the differences of these elements. The solid made of molecules, the house made of bricks, the nervous system made of sensorimotor processes, are nothing more than collections of these practically uniform elements, having certain relations of nextness, and behaviour uniformly depending on that nextness.

The inference of phenomena from phenomena, then, is based upon an assumption of uniformity, which in the present stage of science may be called an atomic uniformity.

The other mode of inference which belongs to the scientific method is that which is used in what are called the mental and moral sciences; and it enables us to go from phenomena to the facts which underlie phenomena, and which are themselves not phenomena at all. If I pinch your arm, and you draw it away and make a face, I infer that you have felt pain. I infer this by assuming that you have a consciousness similar to my own, and related to your perception of your body as my consciousness is related to my perception of my body. Now is this the same assumption as before, a mere assumption of the uniformity of nature? It certainly seems like it at first; but if we think about it we shall find that there is a very profound difference between them. In physical inference I go from phenomena to phenomena; that is, from the knowledge of certain appearances or representations actually present to my mind I infer certain other appearances that might be present to my mind. From the weight of a stone in the morning—that is, from my feeling of its weight, or my perception of the process of weighing it, I infer that the stone will be heavy in the afternoon—that is, I infer the possibility of similar feelings and perceptions in me at another time. The whole process relates to me and my perceptions, to things contained in my mind. But when I infer that you are conscious from what you say or do, I pass from that which is *my* feeling or perception, which is in my mind and part of me, to that which is not my feeling at all, which is outside me altogether, namely, *your* feelings and perceptions. Now there is no possible physical inference, no inference of phenomena from phenomena, that will help me over that gulf. I am obliged to admit that this second kind of inference depends upon another assumption, not included in the assumption of the uniformity of phenomena.

How does a dream differ from waking life? In a fairly coherent dream everything seems quite real, and it is rare, I think, with most people to know in a dream that they are dreaming. Now, if a dream is sufficiently vivid and coherent, all physical inferences are just as valid in it as they are in waking life. In a hazy or imperfect dream, it is true, things melt into one another unexpectedly and unaccountably; we fly, remove mountains, and stop runaway horses with a finger. But there is nothing in the mere nature of a dream to hinder it from being an exact copy of waking experience. If I find a stone heavy in one part of my dream, and infer that it is heavy at some subsequent part, the inference will be verified if the dream is coherent enough; I shall go to the stone, lift it up, and find it as heavy as before. And the same thing is true of all inferences of phenomena from phenomena. For physical purposes a dream is just as good as real life; the only difference is in vividness and coherence.

What, then, hinders us from saying that life is all a dream? If the phenomena we dream of are just as good and real phenomena as those we see and feel when we are awake, what right have we to say that the material universe has any more existence apart from our minds than the things we see and feel in our dreams? The answer which Berkeley[27] gave to that question was, No right at all. The physical universe which I see and feel, and infer, is just my dream and nothing else; that which you see is your dream; only it so happens that all our dreams agree in many respects. This doctrine of Berkeley's has now been so far confirmed by the physiology of the senses, that it is no longer a metaphysical speculation, but a scientifically established fact.[28]

But there is a difference between dreams and waking life, which is of far too great importance for any of us to be in danger of neglecting it. When I see a man in my dream, there is just as good a *body* as if I were awake; muscles, nerves, circulation, capability of adapting means to ends. If only the dream is coherent enough, no physical test can establish that it is a dream. In both cases I see and feel the same thing. In both cases I assume the existence of more than I can see and feel, namely, the consciousness of this other man. But now here is a

---

27 [George Berkeley (1685–1753) was an Irish philosopher. One of his ideas was of immaterialism or subjective idealism, which is a theory that denies the existence of objects and has them as being just ideas in the mind of the observer.]

28 [Dr. Johnson (the famous man of letters) was reported by his biographer to have criticized Berkeley's theory: 'I refute it *thus!*' and kicked a rock with 'mighty force'.]

great difference, and the only difference—in a dream this assumption is wrong; in waking life it is right. The man I see in my dream is a *mere* machine, a bundle of phenomena with no underlying reality; there is no consciousness involved except my consciousness, no feeling in the case except my feelings. The man I see in waking life is more than a bundle of phenomena; his body and its actions are phenomena, but these phenomena are merely the symbols and representatives in my mind of a reality which is outside my mind, namely, the consciousness of the man himself which is represented by the working of his brain, and the simpler quasi-mental facts, not woven into his consciousness, which are represented by the working of the rest of his body. What makes life not to be a dream is the existence of those facts which we arrive at by our second process of inference; the consciousness of men and the higher animals, the sub-consciousness of lower organisms and the quasi-mental facts which go along with the motions of inanimate matter. In a book which is very largely and deservedly known by heart, *Through the Looking-glass*,[29] there is a very instructive discussion upon this point. Alice has been taken to see the Red King as he lies snoring; and Tweedledee asks, 'Do you know what he is dreaming about?' 'Nobody can guess that,' replies Alice. 'Why, about *you*,' he says triumphantly. 'And if he stopped dreaming about you, where do you suppose you'd be?' 'Where I am now of course,' said Alice. 'Not you,' said Tweedledee, 'you'd be nowhere. You are only a sort of thing in his dream.' 'If that there King was to wake,' added Tweedledum, 'you'd go out, bang! just like a candle.' Alice was quite right in regarding these remarks as unphilosophical. The fact that she could see, think, and feel was proof positive that she was not a sort of thing in anybody's dream. This is the meaning of that saying, *Cogito ergo sum*, of Descartes.[30] By him, and by Spinoza[31] after him, the verb *cogito* and the substantive *cogitatio* were used to denote consciousness in general, any kind of feeling, even what we now call sub-consciousness. The saying means that feeling exists in and for itself, not as a quality or modification or state or manifestation of anything else.

---

29 [*Through the Looking-glass, and What Alice Found There* by Lewis Carroll was first published in 1871.]

30 ['I think, therefore I am' first appeared in René Descartes' *Discourse on the Method*, published in 1637. Descartes (1596–1650) was a French philosopher and mathematician.]

31 [Baruch Spinoza (1632–77) was a Dutch philosopher.]

We are obliged in every hour of our lives to act upon beliefs which
have been arrived at by inferences of these two kinds; inferences based
on the assumption of uniformity in nature, and inferences which add
to this the assumption of feelings which are not our own. By organizing the 'common sense' which embodies the first class of inferences,
we build up the physical sciences; that is to say, all those sciences which
deal with the physical, material, or phenomenal universe, whether animate or inanimate. And so by organizing the common sense which
embodies the second class of inferences, we build up various sciences
of mind. The description and classification of feelings, the facts of their
association with each other, and of their simultaneity with phenomena
of nerve-action—all this belongs to psychology, which may be historical and comparative. The doctrine of certain special classes of feelings
is organized into the special sciences of those feelings; thus the facts
about the feelings which we are now considering, about the feelings of
moral approbation and reprobation, are organized into the science of
ethics and the facts about the feeling of beauty or ugliness are organized into the science of aesthetics, or, as it is sometimes called, the
philosophy of art. For all of these the uniformity of nature has to be
assumed as a basis of inference; but over and above that it is necessary to assume that other men are conscious in the same way that I
am. Now in these sciences of mind, just as in the physical sciences, the
uniformity which is assumed in the inferred mental facts is a growing
thing which becomes more definite as we go on, and each successive
generation of observers knows better what to observe and what sort of
inferences may be drawn from observed things. But, moreover, it is as
true of the mental sciences as of the physical ones that the uniformity
is in the present stage of science an *atomic* uniformity. We have learned
to regard our consciousness as made up of elements practically alike,
having relations of succession in time and of contiguity at each instant,
which relations are in all cases practically the same. The element of
consciousness is the transference of an impression into the beginning
of action. Our mental life is a structure made out of such elements, just
as the working of our nervous system is made out of sensorimotor processes. And accordingly the interaction of the two branches of science
leads us to regard the mental facts as the realities or things-in-them-
selves, of which the material phenomena are mere pictures or symbols.
The final result seems to be that atomism is carried beyond phenomena
into the realities which phenomena represent; and that the observed
uniformities of nature, in so far as they can be expressed in the language of atomism, are actual uniformities of things in themselves.

So much for the two things which I have promised to bring together; the facts of our moral feelings, and the scientific method. It may appear that the latter has been expounded at more length than was necessary for the treatment of this particular subject; but the justification for this length is to be found in certain common objections to the claims of science to be the sole judge of mental and moral questions. Some of the chief of these objections I will now mention.

It is sometimes said that science can only deal with what is, but that art and morals deal with what ought to be. The saying is perfectly true, but it is quite consistent with what is equally true, that the facts of art and morals are fit subject-matter of science. I may describe all that I have in my house, and I may state everything that I want in my house; these are two very different things, but they are equally statements of facts. One is a statement about phenomena, about the objects which are actually in my possession; the other is a statement about my feelings, about my wants and desires. There are facts, to be got at by common sense, about the kind of thing that a man of a certain character and occupation will like to have in his house, and these facts may be organized into general statements on the assumption of uniformity in nature. Now the organized results of common sense dealing with facts are just science and nothing else. And in the same way I may say what men do at the present day, how we live now, or I may say what we ought to do, namely, what course of conduct, if adopted, we should morally approve; and no doubt these would be two very different things. But each of them would be a statement of facts. One would belong to the sociology of our time; in so far as men's deeds could not be adequately described to us without some account of their feelings and intentions, it would involve facts belonging to psychology as well as facts belonging to the physical sciences. But the other would be an account of a particular class of our feelings, namely, those which we feel toward an action when it is regarded as right or wrong. These facts may be organized by common sense on the assumption of uniformity in nature just as well as any other facts. And we shall see farther on that not only in this sense, but in a deeper and more abstract sense, 'what ought to be done' is a question for scientific enquiry.

The same objection is sometimes put into another form. It is said that laws of chemistry, for example, are general statements about what happens when bodies are treated in a certain way, and that such laws are fit matter for science; but that moral laws are different, because they tell us to do certain things, and we may or may not obey them. The mood of the one is indicative, of the other imperative. Now it is quite true that the word *law* in the expression 'law of nature,' and in the expressions 'law of morals,' 'law of the land,' has two totally different meanings, which no educated person will confound; and I am not aware that anyone has rested the claim of science to judge moral questions on what is no better than a stale and unprofitable pun. But two different things may be equally matters of scientific investigation, even when their names are alike in sound. A telegraph post is not the same thing as a post in the War Office, and yet the same intelligence may be used to investigate the conditions of the one and the other. That such and such things are right or wrong, that such and such laws are laws of morals or laws of the land, these are facts, just as the laws of chemistry are facts; and all facts belong to science, and are her portion forever.

Again, it is sometimes said that moral questions have been authoritatively settled by other methods; that we ought to accept this decision, and not to question it by any method of scientific enquiry; and that reason should give way to revelation on such matters. I hope before I have done to show just cause why we should pronounce on such teaching as this no light sentence of moral condemnation: first, because it is our duty to form those beliefs which are to guide our actions by the two scientific modes of inference, and by these alone; and, secondly, because the proposed mode of settling ethical questions by authority is contrary to the very nature of right and wrong.

Leaving this, then, for the present, I pass on to the most formidable objection that has been made to a scientific treatment of ethics. The objection is that the scientific method is not applicable to human action, because the rule of uniformity does not hold good. Whenever a man exercises his will, and makes a voluntary choice of one out of various possible courses, an event occurs whose relation to contiguous events cannot be included in a general statement applicable to all similar cases. There is something wholly capricious and disorderly, belonging to that moment only; and we have no right to conclude that if the circumstances were exactly repeated, and the man himself absolutely unaltered, he would choose the same course.

It is clear that if the doctrine here stated is true, the ground is really cut from under our feet, and we cannot deal with human action by the scientific method. I shall endeavour to show, moreover, that in this case, although we might still have a feeling of moral approbation or reprobation toward actions, yet we could not reasonably praise or blame men for their deeds, nor regard them as morally responsible. So that, if my contention is just, to deprive us of the scientific method is practically to deprive us of morals altogether. On both grounds, therefore, it is of the greatest importance that we should define our position in regard to this controversy; if, indeed, that can be called a controversy in which the practical belief of all mankind and the consent of nearly all serious writers are on one side.

Let us in the first place consider a little more closely the connection between conscience and responsibility. Words in common use, such as these two, have their meanings practically fixed before difficult controversies arise; but after the controversy has arisen each party gives that slight tinge to the meaning which best suits its own view of the question. Thus it appears to each that the common language obviously supports their own view, that this is the natural and primary view of the matter, and that the opponents are using words in a new meaning and wrestling them from their proper sense. Now this is just my position. I have endeavoured so far to use all words in their common every-day sense, only making this as precise as I can; and, with two exceptions, of which due warning will be given, I shall do my best to continue this practice in future. I seem to myself to be talking the most obvious platitudes; but it must be remembered that those who take the opposite view will think I am perverting the English language.

There is a common meaning of the word 'responsible,' which though not the same as that of the phrase 'morally responsible,' may throw some light upon it. If we say of a book, 'A is responsible for the preface and the first half, and B is responsible for the rest,' we mean that A wrote the preface and the first half. If two people go into a shop and choose a blue silk dress together, it might be said that A was responsible for its being silk and B for its being blue. Before they chose, the dress was undetermined both in colour and in material. A's choice fixed the material, and then it was undetermined only in colour. B's choice fixed the colour; and if we suppose that there were no more variable conditions (only one blue silk dress in the shop), the dress was then completely determined. In this sense of the word we say that a man is responsible for that part of an event which was undetermined when he was left out of account, and which became determined when he was taken account of. Suppose two narrow streets, one lying north and south, one east and west, and crossing one another. A man is put down where they cross, and has to walk. Then he must walk either north, south, east, or west, and he is not responsible for that; what he is responsible for is the choice of one of these four directions. May we not say in the present sense of the word that the external circumstances are responsible for the restriction on his choice? We should mean only that the fact of his going in one or other of the four directions was due to external circumstances, and not to him. Again, suppose I have a number of punches of various shapes, some square, some oblong, some oval, some round, and that I am going to punch a hole in a piece of paper. *Where* I shall punch the hole may be fixed by any kind of circumstances; but the shape of the hole depends on the punch I take. May we not say that the punch is responsible for the shape of the hole, but not for the position of it?

It may be said that this is not the whole of the meaning of the word 'responsible,' even in its loosest sense; that it ought never to be used except of a conscious agent. Still this is part of its meaning; if we regard an event as determined by a variety of circumstances, a man's choice being among them, we say that he is responsible for just that choice which is left him by the other circumstances.

When we ask the practical question, 'Who is responsible for so-and-so?' we want to find out who is to be got at in order that so-and-so may be altered. If I want to change the shape of the hole I make in my paper, I must change my punch; but this will be of no use if I want to change the position of the hole. If I want the colour of the dress changed from blue to green, it is B, and not A, that I must persuade.

We mean something more than this when we say that a man is *morally* responsible for an action. It seems to me that moral responsibility and conscience go together, both in regard to the man and in regard to the action. In order that a man may be morally responsible for an action, the man must have a conscience, and the action must be one in regard to which conscience is capable of acting as a motive, that is, the action must be capable of being right or wrong. If a child were left on a desert island and grew up wholly without a conscience, and then were brought among men, he would not be morally responsible for his actions until he had acquired a conscience by education. He would of course be *responsible*, in the sense just explained, for that part of them which was left undetermined by external circumstances, and if we wanted to alter his actions in these respects we should have to do it by altering him. But it would be useless and unreasonable to attempt to do this by means of praise or blame, the expression of moral approbation or disapprobation, until he had acquired a conscience which could be worked upon by such means.

It seems, then, that in order that a man may be morally responsible for an action, three things are necessary:

1. He might have done something else; that is to say, the action was not wholly determined by external circumstances, and he is responsible only for the choice which was left him.

2. He had a conscience.
3. The action was one in regard to the doing or not doing of which conscience might be a sufficient motive.

These three things are necessary, but it does not follow that they are sufficient. It is very commonly said that the action must be a *voluntary* one. It will be found, I think, that this is contained in my third condition, and also that the form of statement I have adopted exhibits more clearly the reason why the condition is necessary. We may say that an action is involuntary either when it is instinctive, or when one motive is so strong that there is no voluntary choice between motives. An involuntary cough produced by irritation of the glottis is no proper subject for blame or praise. A man is not responsible for it, because it is done by a part of his body without consulting *him*. What is meant by *him* in this case will require further investigation. Again, when a dipsomaniac has so great and overmastering an inclination to drink that we cannot conceive of conscience being strong enough to conquer it, he is not responsible for that act, though he may be responsible for having got himself into the state. But if it is conceivable that a very strong conscience fully brought to bear might succeed in conquering the inclination, we may take a lenient view of the fall and say there was a very strong temptation, but we shall still regard it as a fall, and say that the man is responsible and a wrong has been done.

But since it is just in this distinction between voluntary and involuntary action that the whole *crux* of the matter lies, let us examine more closely into it. I say that when I cough or sneeze involuntarily, it is really not I that cough or sneeze, but a part of my body which acts without consulting me. This action is determined for me by the circumstances, and is not part of the choice that is left to me, so that I am not responsible for it. The question comes then to determining how much is to be called *circumstances*, and how much is to be called *me*. Now I want to describe what happens when I voluntarily do anything, and there are two courses open to me. I may describe the things in themselves, my feelings and the general course of my consciousness, trusting to the analogy between my consciousness and yours to make me understood; or I may describe these things as nature describes them to your senses, namely in terms of the phenomena of my nervous system, appealing to your memory of phenomena and your knowledge of physical action. I shall do both, because in some respects our knowledge is more complete from the one source, and in some respects from the other. When I look back and reflect upon a voluntary action, I seem to find that it differs from an involuntary action in the fact that a certain portion of my character has been consulted. There is always a suggestion of some sort, either the end of a train of thought or a new sensation; and there is an action ensuing, either the movement of a muscle or set of muscles, or the fixing of attention upon something. But between these two there is a consultation, as it were, of my past history. The suggestion is viewed in the light of everything bearing on it that I think of at the time, and in virtue of this light it moves me to act in one or more ways. Let us first suppose that no hesitation is involved, that only one way of acting is suggested, and I yield to this impulse and act in the particular way. This is the simplest kind of voluntary action. It differs from involuntary or instinctive action in the fact that with the latter there is no such conscious consultation of past history. If we describe these facts in terms of the phenomena which picture them to other minds, we shall say that in involuntary action a message passes straight through from the sensory to the motor centre, and so on to the muscles, without consulting the cerebrum; while involuntary action the message is passed on from the sensory centre to the cerebrum, there translated into appropriate motor stimuli, carried down to the motor centre, and so on to the muscles. There may be other differences, but at least there is this difference. Now on the physical side that which determines, what groups of cerebral fibres shall be set at work by the given message, and what groups of motor stimuli shall be set at work by these, is the mechanism of my brain at the time; and on the mental side that which determines what memories shall be called up by the given sensation, and what motives these memories shall bring into action, is my mental character. We may say, then, in this simplest case of voluntary action, that when the suggestion is given it is the character of *me* which determines the character of the ensuing action; and consequently that I am responsible for choosing that particular course out of those which were left open to me by the external circumstances.

This is when I yield to the impulse. But suppose I do not; suppose that the original suggestion, viewed in the light of memory, sets various motives in action, each motive belonging to a certain class of things which I remember. Then I choose which of these motives shall prevail. Those who carefully watch themselves find out that a particular motive is made to prevail by the fixing of the attention upon that class of remembered things which calls up the motive. The physical side of this is the sending of blood to a certain set of nerves—namely, those whose action corresponds to the memories which are to be attended to. The sending of blood is accomplished by the pinching of arteries;

and there are special nerves, called vasomotor nerves, whose business it is to carry messages to the walls of the arteries and get them pinched. Now this act of directing the attention may be voluntary or involuntary just like any other act. When the transformed and re-enforced nerve-message gets to the vasomotor centre, some part of it may be so predominant that a message goes straight off to the arteries, and sends a quantity of blood to the nerves supplying that part; or the call for blood may be sent back for revision by the cerebrum, which is thus again consulted. To say the same thing in terms of my feelings, a particular class of memories roused by the original suggestion may seize upon my attention before I have time to choose what I will attend to; or the appeal may be carried to a deeper part of my character dealing with wider and more abstract conceptions, which views the conflicting motives in the light of a past experience of motives, and by that light is drawn to one or the other of them.

We thus get to a sort of motive of the second order or motive of motives. Is there any reason why we should not go on to a motive of the third order, and the fourth, and so on? None whatever that I know of, except that no one has ever observed such a thing. There seems plenty of room for the requisite mechanism on the physical side; and no one can say, on the mental side, how complex is the working of his consciousness. But we must carefully distinguish between the intellectual deliberation about motives, which applies to the future and the past, and the practical choice of motives in the moment of will. The former may be a train of any length and complexity: we have no reason to believe that the latter is more than engine and tender.

We are now in a position to classify actions in respect of the kind of responsibility which belongs to them; namely we have:

1. Involuntary or instinctive actions.
2. Voluntary actions in which the choice of motives is involuntary.
3. Voluntary actions in which the choice of motives is voluntary.

In each of these cases what is responsible is that part of my character which determines what the action shall be. For instinctive actions we do not say that *I* am responsible, because the choice is made before I know anything about it. For voluntary actions I am responsible, because I make the choice; that is, the character of me is what determines the character of the action. In *me*, then, for this purpose, is included the aggregate of links of association which determines what memories shall be called up by a given suggestion, and what motives shall be set at work by these memories. But we distinguish this mass of passions and pleasures, desire and knowledge and pain, which makes up most of my character at the moment, from that inner and deeper motive-choosing self which is called Reason, and the Will, and the Ego; which is only responsible when motives are voluntarily chosen by directing attention to them. It is responsible only for the choice of one motive out of those presented to it, not for the nature of the motives which are presented.

But again, I may reasonably be blamed for what I did yesterday, or a week ago, or last year. This is because I am permanent; in so far as from my actions of that date an inference may be drawn about my character now, it is reasonable that I should be treated as praiseworthy or blame-able. And within certain limits I am for the same reason responsible for what I am now, because within certain limits I have made myself. Even instinctive actions are dependent in many cases upon habits which may be altered by proper attention and care; and still more the nature of the connections between sensation and action, the associations of memory and motive, may be voluntarily modified if I choose to try. The habit of choosing among motives is one which may be acquired and strengthened by practice, and the strength of particular motives, by continually directing attention to them, may be almost indefinitely increased or diminished. Thus, if by *me* is meant not the instantane-ous me of this moment, but the aggregate me of my past life, or even of the last year, the range of my responsibility is very largely increased. I am responsible for a very large portion of the circumstances which are now external to me; that is to say, I am responsible for certain of the restrictions on my own freedom. As the eagle was shot with an arrow that flew on its own feather, so I find myself bound with fetters of my proper forging.

Let us now endeavour to conceive an action which is not determined in any way by the character of the agent. If we ask, 'What makes it to be that action and no other?' we are told, 'The man's Ego.' The words are here used, it seems to me, in some non-natural sense, if in any sense at all. One thing makes another to be what it is when the characters of the two things are connected together by some general statement or rule. But we have to suppose that the character of the action is not con-nected with the character of the Ego by any general statement or rule. With the same Ego and the same circumstances of all kinds, anything within the limits imposed by the circumstances may happen at any moment. I find myself unable to conceive any distinct sense in which responsibility could apply in this case; nor do I see at all how it would be reasonable to use praise or blame. If the action does not depend on the character, what is the use of trying to alter the character? Suppose, however, that this indeterminateness is only partial; that the character does add some restrictions to those already imposed by circumstances, but leaves the choice between certain actions undetermined, and to be settled by chance or the transcendental Ego. Is it not clear that the man would be responsible for precisely that part of the character of the action which was determined by his character, and not for what was left undetermined by it? For it is just that part which was determined by his character which it is reasonable to try to alter by altering him.

We who believe in uniformity are not the only people unable to conceive responsibility without it. These are the words of Sir W. Hamilton,[32] as quoted by Mr. J. S. Mill:[33]

> Nay, were we even to admit as true what we cannot think as possible, still the doctrine of a motiveless volition would be only casualism; and the free acts of an indifferent are, morally and rationally, as worthless as the pre-ordered passions of a determined will.
>
> That, though inconceivable, a motiveless volition would, if conceived, be conceived as morally worthless, only shows our impotence more clearly.
>
> Is the person an *original undetermined* cause of the determination of his will? If he be not, then he is not a *free agent*, and the scheme of Necessity is admitted. If he be, in the first place, it is impossible to *conceive* the possibility of this; and in the second, if the fact, though inconceivable, be allowed, it is impossible to see how a cause, undetermined by any motive, can be a rational, moral, and accountable cause.

It is true that Hamilton also says that the scheme of necessity is inconceivable, because it leads to an infinite non-commencement; and that 'the possibility of morality depends on the possibility of liberty; for if a man be not a free agent, he is not the author of his actions, and has, therefore, no responsibility—no moral personality at all.'

I know nothing about necessity; I only believe that nature is practically uniform even in human action. I know nothing about an infinitely distant past; I only know that I ought to base on uniformity those inferences which are to guide my actions. But that man is a free agent

---

32 [Sir William Hamilton (1788–1856) was a Scottish metaphysician. Metaphysics is the part of philosophy that considers the nature of reality.]

33 *Examination*, p. 495, 2d ed. [John Stuart Mill (1806–73) was an English philosopher and the author of *An Examination of Sir William Hamilton's Philosophy*, 1865, among many other books.]

appears to me obvious, and that in the natural sense of the words. We need ask for no better definition than Kant's:[34]

> Will is a kind of causality belonging to living agents, in so far as they are rational; and freedom is such a property of that causality as enables them to be efficient agents independently of outside causes determining them; as, on the other hand, necessity (*Naturnothwendigkeit*) is that property of all irrational beings which consists in their being determined to activity by the influence of outside causes. (*Metaphysics of Ethics*, chap. iii.)

I believe that I am a free agent when my actions are independent of the control of circumstances outside me; and it seems a misuse of language to call me a free agent if my actions are determined by a transcendental Ego who is independent of the circumstances inside me—that is to say, of my character. The expression 'free will' has unfortunately been imported into mental science from a theological controversy rather different from the one we are now considering. It is surely too much to expect that good and serviceable English words should be sacrificed to a phantom.

In an admirable book, *The Methods of Ethics*, Mr. Henry Sidgwick[35] has stated, with supreme fairness and impartiality, both sides of this question. After setting forth the 'almost overwhelming cumulative proof' of uniformity in human action, he says that it seems 'more than balanced by a single argument on the other side: the immediate affirmation of consciousness in the moment of deliberate volition.' 'No amount of experience of the sway of motives ever tends to make me distrust my intuitive consciousness that in resolving, after deliberation, I exercise free choice as to which of the motives acting upon me shall prevail.'

The only answer to this argument is that it is not 'on the other side.' There is no doubt about the deliverance of consciousness; and even if our powers of self-observation had not been acute enough to discover it, the existence of some choice between motives would be proved by the existence of vasomotor nerves. But perhaps the most instructive way of meeting arguments of this kind is to enquire what consciousness ought to say in order that its deliverances may be of any use in

---

34 [Immanuel Kant (1724–1804) was a German philosopher. He is a key figure in modern philosophy.]

35 [Henry Sidgwick (1838–1900) was an English utilitarian philosopher and economist.]

the controversy. It is affirmed, on the side of uniformity, that the feelings in my consciousness in the moment of voluntary choice have been preceded by facts out of my consciousness which are related to them in a uniform manner, so that if the previous facts had been accurately known the voluntary choice might have been predicted. On the other side this is denied. To be of any use in the controversy, then, the immediate deliverance of my consciousness must be competent to assure me of the non-existence of something which by hypothesis is not in my consciousness. Given an absolutely dark room, can my sense of sight assure me that there is no one but myself in it? Can my sense of hearing assure me that nothing inaudible is going on? As little can the immediate deliverance of my consciousness assure me that the uniformity of nature does not apply to human actions.

It is perhaps necessary, in connection with this question, to refer to that singular Materialism of high authority and recent date which makes consciousness a physical agent, 'correlates' it with Light and Nerve-force, and so reduces it to an objective phenomenon. This doctrine is founded on a common and very useful mode of speech, in which we say, for example, that a good fire is a source of pleasure on a cold day, and that a man's feeling of chill may make him run to it. But so also we say that the sun rises and sets every morning and night, although the man in the moon sees clearly that this is due to the rotation of the earth. One cannot be pedantic all day. But if we choose for once to be pedantic, the matter is after all very simple. Suppose that I am made to run by feeling a chill. When I begin to move my leg, I may observe if I like a double series of facts. I have the feeling of effort, the sensation of motion in my leg; I feel the pressure of my foot on the ground. Along with this I may see with my eyes, or feel with my hands, the motion of my leg as a material object. The first series of facts belongs to me alone; the second may be equally observed by anybody else. The mental series began first; I willed to move my leg before I saw it move. But when I know more about the matter, I can trace the material series further back, and find nerve-messages going to the muscles of my leg to make it move. But I had a feeling of chill before I chose to move my leg. Accordingly, I can find nerve-messages, excited by the contraction due to the low temperature, going to my brain from the chilled skin. Assuming the uniformity of nature, I carry forward and backward both the mental and the material series. A uniformity is observed in each, and a parallelism is observed between them, whenever observations can be made. But sometimes one series is known better, and sometimes the other; so that in telling a story we quite naturally speak sometimes of mental facts and sometimes of material facts. A feeling of chill made a man run; strictly speaking, the nervous disturbance which co-existed with that feeling of chill made him run, if we want to talk about material facts; or the feeling of chill produced the form of sub-consciousness which co-exists with the motion of legs, if we want to talk about mental facts. But we know nothing about the special nervous disturbance which co-exists with a feeling of chill, because it has not yet been localized in the brain; and we know nothing about the form of sub-consciousness which co-exists with the motion of legs; although there is very good reason for believing in the existence of both. So we talk about the feeling of chill and the running, because in one case we know the mental side, and in the other the material side. A man might show me a picture of the Battle of Gravelotte,[36] and say, 'You can't see the battle, because it's all over, but there is a picture of it.' And then he might put a Chassepot[37] into my hand, and say, 'We could not represent the whole construction of a Chassepot in the picture, but you can examine this one, and find it out.' If I now insisted on mixing up the two modes of communication of knowledge, if I expected that the Chassepots in the picture would go off, and said that the one in my hand was painted on heavy canvas, I should be acting exactly in the spirit of the new materialism. For the material facts are a representation or symbol of the mental facts, just as a picture is a representation or symbol of a battle. And my own mind is a reality from which I can judge by analogy of the realities represented by other men's brains, just as the Chassepot in my hand is a reality from which I can judge by analogy of the Chassepots represented in the picture. When, therefore, we ask, 'What is the physical link between the ingoing message from chilled skin and the outgoing message which moves the leg?' and the answer is, 'A man's Will,' we have as much right to be amused as if we had asked our friend with the picture what pigment was used in painting the cannon in the foreground, and received the answer, 'Wrought iron.' It will be found excellent practice in the mental operations required by this doctrine to imagine a train, the fore part of which is an engine and three carriages linked with iron couplings, and the hind part three other carriages linked with iron couplings; the

---

36 [Gravelotte is a village in north-east France. On 18 August 1870 the village was the site of the largest battle of the Franco-Prussian War (1870–1).]

37 [A type of French breach-loading rifle used in the Franco-Prussian War. It was a great improvement on the earlier muzzle-loading rifles.]

bond between the two parts being made out of the sentiments of amity subsisting between the stoker and the guard.

To sum up: the uniformity of nature in human actions has been denied on the ground that it takes away responsibility, that it is contradicted by the testimony of consciousness, and that there is a physical correlation between mind and matter. We have replied that the uniformity of nature is necessary to responsibility, that it is affirmed by the testimony of consciousness whenever consciousness is competent to testify, and that matter is the phenomenon or symbol of which mind or quasi-mind is the symbolized and represented thing. We are now free to continue our enquiries on the supposition that nature is uniform.

We began by describing the moral sense of an Englishman. No doubt the description would serve very well for the more civilized nations of Europe; most closely for Germans and Dutch. But the fact that we can speak in this way discloses that there is more than one moral sense, and that what I feel to be right another man may feel to be wrong. Thus we cannot help asking whether there is any reason for preferring one moral sense to another; whether the question, 'What is right to do?' has in any one set of circumstances a single answer which can be definitely known.

Clearly, in the first rough sense of the word, this is not true. What is right for me to do now, seeing that I am here with a certain character, and a certain moral sense as part of it, is just what I feel to be right. The individual conscience is, in the moment of volition, the only possible judge of what is right; there is no conflicting claim. But if we are deliberating about the future, we know that we can modify our conscience gradually by associating with people, reading certain books, and paying attention to certain ideas and feelings; and we may ask ourselves, 'How shall we modify our conscience, if at all? what kind of conscience shall we try to get? what is the *best* conscience?' We may ask similar questions about our sense of taste. There is no doubt at present that the nicest things to me are the things I like; but I know that I can train myself to like some things and dislike others, and that things which are very nasty at one time may come to be great delicacies at another. I may ask, 'How shall I train myself? What is the *best* taste?' And this leads very naturally to putting the question in another form, namely, 'What is taste good for? What is the *purpose* or *function* of taste?' We should probably find as the answer to that question that the purpose or function of taste is to discriminate wholesome food from unwholesome; that it is a matter of stomach and digestion. It will follow from this that the best taste is that which prefers wholesome food, and that by cultivating a preference for wholesome and nutritious things I shall be training my palate in the way it should go. In just the same way our question about the best conscience will resolve itself into a question about the purpose or function of the conscience—why we have got it, and what it is good for.

Now to my mind the simplest and clearest and most profound philosophy that was ever written upon this subject is to be found in the second and third chapters of Mr. Darwin's *Descent of Man*.[38] In these chapters it appears that just as most physical characteristics of organisms have been evolved and preserved because they were useful to the individual in the struggle for existence against other individuals and other species, so this particular feeling has been evolved and preserved because it is useful to the tribe or community in the struggle for existence against other tribes, and against the environment as a whole. The function of conscience is the preservation of the tribe as a tribe. And we shall rightly train our consciences if we learn to approve those actions which tend to the advantage of the community in the struggle for existence.

There are here some words, however, which require careful definition. And first the word *purpose*. A thing serves a purpose when it is adapted to some end; thus a corkscrew is adapted to the end of extracting corks from bottles, and our lungs are adapted to the end of respiration. We may say that the extraction of corks is the purpose of the corkscrew, and that respiration is the purpose of the lungs. But here we shall have used the word in two different senses. A man made the corkscrew with a purpose in his mind, and he knew and intended that it should be used for pulling out corks. But nobody made our lungs with a purpose in his mind, and intended that they should be used for breathing. The respiratory apparatus was adapted to its purpose by natural selection— namely, by the gradual preservation of better and better adaptations, and the killing off of the worse and imperfect adaptations. In using the word purpose for the result of this unconscious process of adaptation by survival of the fittest, I know that I am somewhat extending its ordinary sense, which implies consciousness. But it seems to me that on the score of convenience there is a great deal to be said for this extension of meaning. We want a word to express the adaptation of means to an end, whether involving consciousness or not; the word purpose

---

38 [Charles Darwin (1809–82), *The Descent of Man and Selection in Relation to Sex*, 1871.]

will do very well, and the adjective *purposive* has already been used in this sense. But if the use is admitted, we must distinguish two kinds of purpose. There is the unconscious purpose which is attained by natural selection, in which no consciousness need be concerned; and there is the conscious purpose of an intelligence which designs a thing that it may serve to do something which he desires to be done. The distinguishing mark of this second kind, design or conscious purpose, is that in the consciousness of the agent there is an image or symbol of the end which he desires, and this precedes and determines the use of the means. Thus the man who first invented a corkscrew must have previously known that corks were in bottles, and have desired to get them out. We may describe this if we like in terms of matter, and say that a purpose of the second kind implies a complex nervous system, in which there can be formed an image or symbol of the end, and that this symbol determines the use of the means. The nervous image or symbol of anything is that mode of working of part of my brain which goes on simultaneously and is correlated with my thinking of the thing.

Aristotle[39] defines an organism as that in which the part exists for the sake of the whole. It is not that the existence of the part depends on the existence of the whole, for every whole exists only as an aggregate of parts related in a certain way; but that the shape and nature of the part are determined by the wants of the whole. Thus the shape and nature of my foot are what they are, not for the sake of my foot itself, but for the sake of my whole body, and because it wants to move about. That which the part has to do for the whole is called its function. Thus the function of my foot is to support me, and assist in locomotion. Not all the nature of the part is necessarily for the sake of the whole: the comparative callosity of the skin of my sole is for the protection of my foot itself.

Society is an organism, and man in society is part of an organism according to this definition, in so far as some portion of the nature of man is what it is for the sake of the whole—society. Now conscience is such a portion of the nature of man, and its function is the preservation of society in the struggle for existence. We may be able to define this function more closely when we know more about the way in which conscience tends to preserve society.

Next let us endeavour to make precise the meaning of the words *community* and *society*. It is clear that at different times men may be divided into groups of greater or less extent—tribes, clans, families,

---

39 [An Ancient Greek philosopher (BC 384–322).]

nations, towns. If a certain number of clans are struggling for existence, that portion of the conscience will be developed which tends to
the preservation of the clan; so, if towns or families are struggling, we
shall get a moral sense adapted to the advantage of the town or the family. In this way different portions of the moral sense may be developed
at different stages of progress. Now it is clear that for the purpose of the
conscience the word community at any time will mean a group of that
size and nature which is being selected or not selected for survival as a
whole. Selection may be going on at the same time among many different kinds of groups. And ultimately the moral sense will be composed
of various portions relating to various groups, the function or purpose
of each portion being the advantage of that group to which it relates
in the struggle for existence. Thus we have a sense of family duty, of
municipal duty, of national duty, and of duties toward all mankind.

It is to be noticed that part of the nature of a smaller group may be
what it is for the sake of a larger group to which it belongs; and then we
may speak of the *function* of the smaller group. Thus it appears probable that the family, in the form in which it now exists among us, is
determined by the good of the nation; and we may say that the function of the family is to promote the advantage of the nation or larger
society in some certain ways. But I do not think it would be right to follow Auguste Comte[40] in speaking of the function of humanity; because
humanity is obviously not a part of any larger organism for whose sake
it is what it is.

Now that we have cleared up the meanings of some of our words, we
are still a great way from the definite solution of our question, 'What
is the best conscience? or what ought I to think right?' For we do not
yet know what is for the advantage of the community in the struggle for existence. If we choose to learn by the analogy of an individual
organism, we may see that no permanent or final answer can be given,
because the organism grows in consequence of the struggle, and devel-
ops new wants while it is satisfying the old ones. But at any given time
it has quite enough to do to keep alive and to avoid dangers and diseases. So we may expect that the wants and even the necessities of the
social organism will grow with its growth, and that it is impossible
to predict what may tend in the distant future to its advantage in the

---

40 [Isidore Marie Auguste François Xavier Comte (1798–1857) was a French philosopher. He founded the discipline of praxeology, which is the study of human
action based on the idea that humans engage in purposeful behaviour.]

struggle for existence. But still, in this vague and general statement of the functions of conscience, we shall find that we have already established a great deal.

In the first place, right is an affair of the community, and must not be referred to anything else. To go back to our analogy of taste: if I tried to persuade you that the best palate was that which preferred things pretty to look at, you might condemn me *a priori* without any experience, by merely knowing that taste is an affair of stomach and digestion—that its function is to select wholesome food. And so, if anyone tries to persuade us that the best conscience is that which thinks it right to obey the will of some individual, as a deity or a monarch, he is condemned *a priori* in the very nature of right and wrong. In order that the worship of a deity may be consistent with natural ethics, he must be regarded as the friend and helper of humanity, and his character must be judged from his actions by a moral standard which is independent of him. And this, it must be admitted, is the position which has been taken by most English divines, as long as they were Englishmen first and divines afterward. The worship of a deity who is represented as unfair or unfriendly to any portion of the community is a wrong thing, however great may be the threats and promises by which it is commended. And still worse, the reference of right and wrong to his arbitrary will as a standard, the diversion of the allegiance of the moral sense from the community to him, is the most insidious and fatal of social diseases. It was against this that the Teutonic conscience protested in the Reformation. Again, in monarchical countries, in order that allegiance to the sovereign may be consistent with natural ethics, he must be regarded as the servant and symbol of the national unity, capable of rebellion and punishable for it. And this has been the theory of the English constitution from time immemorial.

The first principle of natural ethics, then, is the sole and supreme allegiance of conscience to the community. I venture to call this *piety* in accordance with the older meaning of the word. Even if it should turn out impossible to sever it from the unfortunate associations which have clung to its later meaning, still it seems worthwhile to try.

An immediate deduction from our principle is that there are no self-regarding virtues properly so called; those qualities which tend to the advantage and preservation of the individual being only morally *right* in so far as they make him a more useful citizen. And this conclusion is in some cases of great practical importance. The virtue of purity, for example, attains in this way a fairly exact definition: purity in a man is that course of conduct which makes him to be a good husband and father, in a woman that which makes her to be a good wife and mother, or which helps other people so to prepare and keep themselves. It is easy to see how many false ideas and pernicious precepts are swept away by even so simple a definition as that.

Next, we may fairly define our position in regard to that moral system which has deservedly found favour with the great mass of our countrymen. In the common statement of utilitarianism the end of right action is defined to be the greatest happiness of the greatest number. It seems to me that the reason and the ample justification of the success of this system is that it explicitly sets forth the community as the object of moral allegiance. But our determination of the purpose of the conscience will oblige us to make a change in the statement of it. Happiness is not the end of right action. My happiness is of no use to the community except in so far as it makes me a more efficient citizen; that is to say, it is rightly desired as a means and not as an end. The end may be described as the greatest efficiency of all citizens as such. No doubt happiness will in the long run accrue to the community as a consequence of right conduct; but the right is determined independently of the happiness, and, as Plato says, it is better to suffer wrong than to do wrong.

In conclusion, I would add some words on the relation of Veracity to the first principle of Piety. It is clear that veracity is founded on faith in man; you tell a man the truth when you can trust him with it and are not afraid. This perhaps is made more evident by considering the case of exception allowed by all moralists—namely, that if a man asks you the way with a view to committing a murder, it is right to tell a lie and misdirect him. The reason why he must not have the truth told him is that he would make a bad use of it; he cannot be trusted with it. About these cases of exception an important remark must be made in passing. When we hear that a man has told a lie under such circumstances, we are indeed ready to admit that for once it was right, *mensonge admirable*;[41] but we always have a sort of feeling that it must not occur again. And the same thing applies to cases of conflicting obligations, when for example the family conscience and the national conscience disagree. In such cases no general rule can be laid down; we have to choose the less of two evils; but this is not right altogether in the same sense as it is right to speak the truth. There is something wrong in the circumstances, that we should have to choose an evil at all. The

---

41 ['Admirable lie.']

actual course to be pursued will vary with the progress of society; that evil which at first was greater will become less, and in a perfect society the conflict will be resolved into harmony. But meanwhile these cases of exception must be carefully kept distinct from the straightforward cases of right and wrong, and they always imply an obligation to mend the circumstances if we can.

Veracity to an individual is not only enjoined by piety in virtue of the obvious advantage which attends a straightforward and mutually trusting community as compared with others, but also because deception is in all cases a personal injury. Still more is this true of veracity to the community itself. The conception of the universe or aggregate of beliefs which forms the link between sensation and action for each individual is a public and not a private matter; it is formed by society and for society. Of what enormous importance it is to the community that this should be a true conception I need not attempt to describe. Now to the attainment of this true conception two things are necessary.

First, if we study the history of those methods by which true beliefs and false beliefs have been attained, we shall see that it is our duty to guide our beliefs by inference from experience on the assumption of uniformity of nature and consciousness in other men, *and by this only*. Only upon this moral basis can the foundations of the empirical method be justified.

Secondly, veracity to the community depends upon faith in man. Surely I ought to be talking platitudes when I say that it is not English to tell a man a lie, or to suggest a lie by your silence or your actions, because you are afraid that he is not prepared for the truth, because you don't quite know what he will do when he knows it, because perhaps after all this lie is a better thing for him than the truth would be, this same man being all the time an honest fellow-citizen whom you have every reason to trust. Surely I have heard that this craven crookedness is the object of our national detestation. And yet it is constantly whispered that it would be dangerous to divulge certain truths to the masses. 'I know the whole thing is untrue: but then it is so useful for the people; you don't know what harm you might do by shaking their faith in it.' Crooked ways are none the less crooked because they are meant to deceive great masses of people instead of individuals. If a thing is true, let us all believe it, rich and poor, men, women, and children. If a thing is untrue, let us all disbelieve it, rich and poor, men, women, and children. Truth is a thing to be shouted from the housetops, not to be whispered over rose-water after dinner when the ladies are gone away.

Even in those whom I would most reverence, who would shrink with horror from such actual deception as I have just mentioned, I find traces of a want of faith in man. Even that noble thinker, to whom we of this generation owe more than I can tell, seemed to say in one of his posthumous essays that in regard to questions of great public importance we might encourage a hope in excess of the evidence (which would infallibly grow into a belief and defy evidence) if we found that life was made easier by it. As if we should not lose infinitely more by nourishing a tendency to falsehood than we could gain by the delusion of a pleasing fancy. Life must first of all be made straight and true; it may get easier through the help this brings to the commonwealth. And Lange, the great historian of materialism, says that the amount of false belief necessary to morality in a given society is a matter of taste. I cannot believe that any falsehood whatever is necessary to morality. It cannot be true of my race and yours that to keep ourselves from becoming scoundrels we must needs believe a lie. The sense of right grew up among healthy men and was fixed by the practice of comradeship. It has never had help from phantoms and falsehoods, and it never can want any. By faith in man and piety toward men we have taught each other the right hitherto; with faith in man and piety toward men we shall never more depart from it.

3. The Ethics of Belief

I. The Duty of Enquiry

A SHIPOWNER WAS ABOUT TO send to sea an emigrant-ship. He knew that she was old, and not over-well built at the first; that she had seen many seas and climes, and often had needed repairs. Doubts had been suggested to him that possibly she was not seaworthy. These doubts preyed upon his mind, and made him unhappy; he thought that perhaps he ought to have her thoroughly overhauled and refitted, even though this should put him to great expense. Before the ship sailed, however, he succeeded in overcoming these melancholy reflections. He said to himself that she had gone safely through so many voyages and weathered so many storms that it was idle to suppose she would not come safely home from this trip also. He would put his trust in Providence, which could hardly fail to protect all these unhappy families that were leaving their fatherland to seek for better times elsewhere. He would dismiss from his mind all ungenerous suspicions about the honesty of builders and contractors. In such ways he acquired a sincere and comfortable conviction that his vessel was thoroughly safe and seaworthy; he watched her departure with a light heart, and benevolent wishes for the success of the exiles in their strange new home that was to be; and he got his insurance-money when she went down in mid-ocean and told no tales.

What shall we say of him? Surely this, that he was verily guilty of the death of those men. It is admitted that he did sincerely believe in the soundness of his ship; but the sincerity of his conviction can in no wise help him, because *he had no right to believe on such evidence as was before him*. He had acquired his belief not by honestly earning it in patient investigation, but by stifling his doubts. And although in the end he may have felt so sure about it that he could not think otherwise, yet inasmuch as he had knowingly and willingly worked himself into that frame of mind, he must be held responsible for it.

Let us alter the case a little, and suppose that the ship was not unsound after all; that she made her voyage safely, and many others after it. Will that diminish the guilt of her owner? Not one jot. When an action is once done, it is right or wrong forever; no accidental failure of its good or evil fruits can possibly alter that. The man would not have been innocent, he would only have been not found out. The question of right or wrong has to do with the origin of his belief, not the matter of it; not what it was, but how he got it; not whether it turned out to be true or false, but whether he had a right to believe on such evidence as was before him.

There was once an island in which some of the inhabitants professed a religion teaching neither the doctrine of original sin nor that of eternal punishment. A suspicion got abroad that the professors of this religion had made use of unfair means to get their doctrines taught to children. They were accused of wresting the laws of their country in such a way as to remove children from the care of their natural and legal guardians; and even of stealing them away and keeping them concealed from their friends and relations. A certain number of men formed themselves into a society for the purpose of agitating the public about this matter. They published grave accusations against individual citizens of the highest position and character, and did all in their power to injure these citizens in the exercise of their professions. So great was the noise they made, that a Commission was appointed to investigate the facts; but after the Commission had carefully enquired into all the evidence that could be got, it appeared that the accused were innocent. Not only had they been accused on insufficient evidence, but the evidence of their innocence was such as the agitators might easily have obtained, if they had attempted a fair enquiry. After these disclosures the inhabitants of that country looked upon the members of the agitating society, not only as persons whose judgement was to be distrusted, but also as no longer to be counted honourable men. For although they had sincerely and conscientiously believed in the charges they had made, yet *they had no right to believe on such evidence as was before them.* Their sincere convictions, instead of being honestly earned by patient inquiring, were stolen by listening to the voice of prejudice and passion.

Let us vary this case also, and suppose, other things remaining as before, that a still more accurate investigation proved the accused to have been really guilty. Would this make any difference in the guilt of the accusers? Clearly not; the question is not whether their belief was true or false, but whether they entertained it on wrong grounds. They would no doubt say, 'Now you see that we were right after all; next time perhaps you will believe us.' And they might be believed, but they would not thereby become honourable men. They would not be innocent, they would only be not found out. Every one of them, if he chose to examine himself *in foro conscientiae*,[42] would know that he had acquired and nourished a belief, when he had no right to believe on such evidence as was before him; and therein he would know that he had done a wrong thing.

It may be said, however, that in both of these supposed cases it is not the belief which is judged to be wrong, but the action following upon it. The shipowner might say, 'I am perfectly certain that my ship is sound, but still I feel it my duty to have her examined, before trusting the lives of so many people to her.' And it might be said to the agitator, 'However convinced you were of the justice of your cause and the truth of your convictions, you ought not to have made a public attack upon any man's character until you had examined the evidence on both sides with the utmost patience and care.'

In the first place, let us admit that, so far as it goes, this view of the case is right and necessary; right, because even when a man's belief is so fixed that he cannot think otherwise, he still has a choice in regard to the action suggested by it, and so cannot escape the duty of investigating on the ground of the strength of his convictions; and necessary, because those who are not yet capable of controlling their feelings and thoughts must have a plain rule dealing with overt acts.

But this being premised as necessary, it becomes clear that it is not sufficient, and that our previous judgement is required to supplement it. For it is not possible so to sever the belief from the action it suggests as to condemn the one without condemning the other. No man holding a strong belief on one side of a question, or even wishing to hold a belief on one side, can investigate it with such fairness and completeness as if he were really in doubt and unbiased; so that the existence of a belief not founded on fair enquiry unfits a man for the performance of this necessary duty.

Nor is that truly a belief at all which has not some influence upon the actions of him who holds it. He who truly believes that which prompts him to an action has looked upon the action to lust after it, he has committed it already in his heart. If a belief is not realized immediately in open deeds, it is stored up for the guidance of the future. It goes to make a part of that aggregate of beliefs which is the link between sensation and action at every moment of all our lives, and which is so organized and compacted together that no part of it can be isolated from the rest, but every new addition modifies the structure of the whole. No

---

42 [Privately or morally rather than legally.]

real belief, however trifling and fragmentary it may seem, is ever truly insignificant; it prepares us to receive more of its like, confirms those which resembled it before, and weakens others; and so gradually it lays a stealthy train in our inmost thoughts, which may some day explode into overt action, and leave its stamp upon our character forever.

And no one man's belief is in any case a private matter which concerns himself alone. Our lives are guided by that general conception of the course of things which has been created by society for social purposes. Our words, our phrases, our forms and processes and modes of thought, are common property, fashioned and perfected from age to age; an heirloom which every succeeding generation inherits as a precious deposit and a sacred trust to be handed on to the next one, not unchanged but enlarged and purified, with some clear marks of its proper handiwork. Into this, for good or ill, is woven every belief of every man who has speech of his fellows. An awful privilege, and an awful responsibility, that we should help to create the world in which posterity will live.

In the two supposed cases which have been considered, it has been judged wrong to believe on insufficient evidence, or to nourish belief by suppressing doubts and avoiding investigation. The reason of this judgement is not far to seek: it is that in both these cases the belief held by one man was of great importance to other men. But forasmuch as no belief held by one man, however seemingly trivial the belief, and however obscure the believer, is ever actually insignificant or without its effect on the fate of mankind, we have no choice but to extend our judgement to all cases of belief whatever. Belief, that sacred faculty which prompts the decisions of our will, and knits into harmonious working all the compacted energies of our being, is ours not for ourselves, but for humanity. It is rightly used on truths which have been established by long experience and waiting toil, and which have stood in the fierce light of free and fearless questioning. Then it helps to bind men together, and to strengthen and direct their common action. It is desecrated when given to unproved and unquestioned statements, for the solace and private pleasure of the believer; to add a tinsel splendour to the plain straight road of our life and display a bright mirage beyond it; or even to drown the common sorrows of our kind by a self-deception which allows them not only to cast down, but also to degrade us. Whoso would deserve well of his fellows in this matter will guard the purity of his belief with a very fanaticism of jealous care, lest at any time it should rest on an unworthy object, and catch a stain which can never be wiped away.

It is not only the leader of men, statesman, philosopher, or poet, that owes this bounden duty to mankind. Every rustic who delivers in the village alehouse his slow, infrequent sentences, may help to kill or keep alive the fatal superstitions which clog his race. Every hard-worked wife of an artisan may transmit to her children beliefs which shall knit society together, or rend it in pieces. No simplicity of mind, no obscurity of station, can escape the universal duty of questioning all that we believe.

It is true that this duty is a hard one, and the doubt which comes out of it is often a very bitter thing. It leaves us bare and powerless where we thought that we were safe and strong. To know all about anything is to know how to deal with it under all circumstances. We feel much happier and more secure when we think we know precisely what to do, no matter what happens, than when we have lost our way and do not know where to turn. And if we have supposed ourselves to know all about anything, and to be capable of doing what is fit in regard to it, we naturally do not like to find that we are really ignorant and powerless, that we have to begin again at the beginning, and try to learn what the thing is and how it is to be dealt with—if indeed anything can be learnt about it. It is the sense of power attached to a sense of knowledge that makes men desirous of believing, and afraid of doubting.

This sense of power is the highest and best of pleasures when the belief on which it is founded is a true belief, and has been fairly earned by investigation. For then we may justly feel that it is common property, and holds good for others as well as for ourselves. Then we may be glad, not that *I* have learned secrets by which I am safer and stronger, but that *we men* have got mastery over more of the world; and we shall be strong, not for ourselves, but in the name of Man and in his strength. But if the belief has been accepted on insufficient evidence, the pleasure is a stolen one. Not only does it deceive ourselves by giving us a sense of power which we do not really possess, but it is sinful, because it is stolen in defiance of our duty to mankind. That duty is to guard ourselves from such beliefs as from a pestilence, which may shortly master our own body and then spread to the rest of the town. What would be thought of one who, for the sake of a sweet fruit, should deliberately run the risk of bringing a plague upon his family and his neighbours?

And, as in other such cases, it is not the risk only which has to be considered; for a bad action is always bad at the time when it is done, no matter what happens afterward. Every time we let ourselves believe for unworthy reasons, we weaken our powers of self-control, of doubting, of judicially and fairly weighing evidence. We all suffer severely enough from the maintenance and support of false beliefs and the fatally wrong actions which they lead to, and the evil born when one such belief is entertained is great and wide. But a greater and wider evil arises when the credulous character is maintained and supported, when a habit of believing for unworthy reasons is fostered and made permanent. If I steal money from any person, there may be no harm done by the mere transfer of possession; he may not feel the loss, or it may prevent him from using the money badly. But I cannot help doing this great wrong toward Man, that I make myself dishonest. What hurts society is not that it should lose its property, but that it should become a den of thieves; for then it must cease to be society. This is why we ought not to do evil that good may come; for at any rate this great evil has come, that we have done evil and are made wicked thereby. In like manner, if I let myself believe anything on insufficient evidence, there may be no great harm done by the mere belief; it may be true after all, or I may never have occasion to exhibit it in outward acts. But I cannot help doing this great wrong toward Man, that I make myself credulous. The danger to society is not merely that it should believe wrong things, though that is great enough; but that it should become credulous, and lose the habit of testing things and inquiring into them; for then it must sink back into savagery.

The harm which is done by credulity in a man is not confined to the fostering of a credulous character in others, and consequent support of false beliefs. Habitual want of care about what I believe leads to habitual want of care in others about the truth of what is told to me. Men speak the truth to one another when each reveres the truth in his own mind and in the other's mind; but how shall my friend revere the truth in my mind when I myself am careless about it, when I believe things because I want to believe them, and because they are comforting and pleasant? Will he not learn to cry, 'Peace,' to me, when there is no peace? By such a course I shall surround myself with a thick atmosphere of falsehood and fraud, and in that I must live. It may matter little to me, in my cloud-castle of sweet illusions and darling lies; but it matters much to Man that I have made my neighbours ready to deceive. The credulous man is father to the liar and the cheat; he lives in the bosom of this his family, and it is no marvel if he should become even as they are. So closely are our duties knit together, that whoso shall keep the whole law, and yet offend in one point, he is guilty of all.

To sum up: it is wrong always, everywhere and for anyone, to believe anything upon insufficient evidence.

If a man, holding a belief which he was taught in childhood or per-suaded of afterward, keeps down and pushes away any doubts which arise about it in his mind, purposely avoids the reading of books and the company of men that call in question or discuss it, and regards as impious those questions which cannot easily be asked without disturbing it—the life of that man is one long sin against mankind.

If this judgement seems harsh when applied to those simple souls who have never known better, who have been brought up from the cradle with a horror of doubt, and taught that their eternal welfare depends on *what* they believe, then it leads to the very serious question, *Who hath made Israel to sin?*[43]

It may be permitted me to fortify this judgement with the sentence of Milton:[44]

> A man may be a heretic in the truth; and if he believe things only because his pastor says so, or the assembly so determine, without knowing other reason, though his belief be true, yet the very truth he holds becomes his heresy.[45]

And with this famous aphorism of Coleridge:[46]

> He who begins by loving Christianity better than Truth, will proceed by loving his own sect or Church better than Christianity, and end in loving himself better than all.[47]

Enquiry into the evidence of a doctrine is not to be made once for all, and then taken as finally settled. It is never lawful to stifle a doubt; for either it can be honestly answered by means of the enquiry already made, or else it proves that the enquiry was not complete.

'But,' says one, 'I am a busy man; I have no time for the long course of study which would be necessary to make me in any degree a competent judge of certain questions, or even able to understand the nature of the arguments.' Then he should have no time to believe.

---

43 [King James Bible: 1 Kings 14:16: 'And he shall give Israel up because of the sins of Jeroboam, who did sin, and who made Israel to sin.']

44 [John Milton (1608–74) was an English poet and literarist. His is most famous for his poem *Paradise Lost* (1667).]

45 [From *Areopagitica; A speech of Mr. John Milton for the Liberty of Unlicenc'd Printing, to the Parlament of England*, 1644. Milton wrote this to oppose licensing and censorship.]

46 [Samuel Taylor Coleridge (1772–1834) was an English poet, literarist and philosopher.]

47 [From Coleridge's *Aids to Reflection* (1873), Aphorism XXV.]

II. The Weight of Authority

Are we then to become universal sceptics, doubting everything, afraid always to put one foot before the other until we have personally tested the firmness of the road? Are we to deprive ourselves of the help and guidance of that vast body of knowledge which is daily growing upon the world, because neither we nor any other one person can possibly test a hundredth part of it by immediate experiment or observation, and because it would not be completely proved if we did? Shall we steal and tell lies because we have had no personal experience wide enough to justify the belief that it is wrong to do so?

There is no practical danger that such consequences will ever follow from scrupulous care and self-control in the matter of belief. Those men who have most nearly done their duty in this respect have found that certain great principles, and these most fitted for the guidance of life, have stood out more and more clearly in proportion to the care and honesty with which they were tested, and have acquired in this way a practical certainty. The beliefs about right and wrong which guide our actions in dealing with men in society, and the beliefs about physical nature which guide our actions in dealing with animate and inanimate bodies, these never suffer from investigation; they can take care of themselves, without being propped up by 'acts of faith,' the clamour of paid advocates, or the suppression of contrary evidence. Moreover there are many cases in which it is our duty to act upon probabilities, although the evidence is not such as to justify present belief; because it is precisely by such action, and by observation of its fruits, that evidence is got which may justify future belief. So that we have no reason to fear lest a habit of conscientious enquiry should paralyse the actions of our daily life.

But because it is not enough to say, 'It is wrong to believe on unworthy evidence,' without saying also what evidence is worthy, we shall now go on to enquire under what circumstances it is lawful to believe on the testimony of others; and then, further, we shall enquire more generally when and why we may believe that which goes beyond our own experience, or even beyond the experience of mankind.

In what cases, then, let us ask in the first place, is the testimony of a man unworthy of belief? He may say that which is untrue either knowingly or unknowingly. In the first case he is lying, and his moral character is to blame; in the second case he is ignorant or mistaken, and it is only his knowledge or his judgement which is in fault. In order that we may have the right to accept his testimony as ground for believing what he says, we must have reasonable grounds for trusting his *veracity*, that he is really trying to speak the truth so far as he knows it; his *knowledge*, that he has had opportunities of knowing the truth about this matter; and his *judgement*, that he has made proper use of those opportunities in coming to the conclusion which he affirms.

However plain and obvious these reasons may be, so that no man of ordinary intelligence, reflecting upon the matter, could fail to arrive at them, it is nevertheless true that a great many persons do habitually disregard them in weighing testimony. Of the two questions, equally important to the trustworthiness of a witness, 'Is he dishonest?' and 'May he be mistaken?' the majority of mankind are perfectly satisfied if *one* can, with some show of probability, be answered in the negative. The excellent moral character of a man is alleged as ground for accepting his statements about things which he cannot possibly have known. A Muhammadan, for example, will tell us that the character of his Prophet was so noble and majestic that it commands the reverence even of those who do not believe in his mission. So admirable was his moral teaching, so wisely put together the great social machine which he created, that his precepts have not only been accepted by a great portion of mankind, but have actually been obeyed. His institutions have on the one hand rescued the negro from savagery, and on the other hand have taught civilization to the advancing West; and although the races which held the highest forms of his faith, and most fully embodied his mind and thought, have all been conquered and swept away by barbaric tribes, yet the history of their marvellous attainments remains as an imperishable glory to Islam. Are we to doubt the word of a man so great and so good? Can we suppose that this magnificent genius, this splendid moral hero, has lied to us about the most solemn and sacred matters? The testimony of Muhammad is clear, that there is but one God, and that he, Muhammad, is his prophet; that if we believe in him we shall enjoy everlasting felicity, but that if we do not we shall be damned. This testimony rests on the most awful of foundations, the revelation of heaven itself; for was he not visited by the angel Gabriel, as he fasted and prayed in his desert cave, and allowed to enter into the blessed fields of Paradise? Surely God is God and Muhammad is the Prophet of God.

What should we answer to this Muslim? First, no doubt, we should be tempted to take exception against his view of the character of the Prophet and the uniformly beneficial influence of Islam: before we could go with him altogether in these matters it might seem that we should have to forget many terrible things of which we have heard or read. But if we chose to grant him all these assumptions, for the sake of argument, and because it is difficult both for the faithful and for infidels to discuss them fairly and without passion, still we should have something to say which takes away the ground of his belief, and therefore shows that it is wrong to entertain it. Namely this: the character of Muhammad is excellent evidence that he was honest and spoke the truth so far as he knew it; but it is no evidence at all that he knew what the truth was. What means could he have of knowing that the form which appeared to him to be the angel Gabriel was not a hallucination, and that his apparent visit to Paradise was not a dream? Grant that he himself was fully persuaded and honestly believed that he had the guidance of heaven, and was the vehicle of a supernatural revelation, how could he know that this strong conviction was not a mistake? Let us put ourselves in his place; we shall find that the more completely we endeavour to realize what passed through his mind, the more clearly we shall perceive that the Prophet could have had no adequate ground for the belief in his own inspiration. It is most probable that he himself never doubted of the matter, or thought of asking the question; but we are in the position of those to whom the question has been asked, and who are bound to answer it. It is known to medical observers that solitude and want of food are powerful means of producing delusion and of fostering a tendency to mental disease. Let us suppose, then, that I, like Muhammad, go into desert places to fast and pray; what things can happen to me which will give me the right to believe that I am divinely inspired? Suppose that I get information, apparently from a celestial visitor, which upon being tested is found to be correct. I cannot be sure, in the first place, that the celestial visitor is not a figment of my own mind, and that the information did not come to me, unknown at the time to my consciousness, through some subtle channel of sense. But if my visitor were a real visitor, and for a long time gave me information which was found to be trustworthy, this would indeed be good ground for trusting him in the future as to such matters as fall within human powers of verification; but it would not be ground for trusting his testimony as to any other matters. For although his tested character would justify me in believing that he spoke the truth so far as he knew, yet the same question would present itself—what ground is there for supposing that he knows?

Even if my supposed visitor had given me such information, subsequently verified by me, as proved him to have means of knowledge about verifiable matters far exceeding my own; this would not justify me in believing what he said about matters that are not at present capable of verification by man. It would be ground for interesting conjecture, and for the hope that, as the fruit of our patient enquiry, we might by and by attain to such a means of verification as should rightly turn conjecture into belief. For belief belongs to man, and to the guidance of human affairs: no belief is real unless it guide our actions, and those very actions supply a test of its truth.

But, it may be replied, the acceptance of Islam as a system is just that action which is prompted by belief in the mission of the Prophet, and which will serve for a test of its truth. Is it possible to believe that a system which has succeeded so well is really founded upon a delusion? Not only have individual saints found joy and peace in believing, and verified those spiritual experiences which are promised to the faithful, but nations also have been raised from savagery or barbarism to a higher social state. Surely we are at liberty to say that the belief has been acted upon, and that it has been verified.

It requires, however, but little consideration to show that what has really been verified is not at all the supernal character of the Prophet's mission, or the trustworthiness of his authority in matters which we ourselves cannot test, but only his practical wisdom in certain very mundane things. The fact that believers have found joy and peace in believing gives us the right to say that the doctrine is a comfortable doctrine, and pleasant to the soul; but it does not give us the right to say that it is true. And the question which our conscience is always asking about that which we are tempted to believe is not, 'Is it comfortable and pleasant?' but, 'Is it true?' That the Prophet preached certain doctrines, and predicted that spiritual comfort would be found in them, proves only his sympathy with human nature and his knowledge of it; but it does not prove his superhuman knowledge of theology.

And if we admit for the sake of argument (for it seems that we cannot do more) that the progress made by Muslim nations in certain cases was really due to the system formed and sent forth into the world by Muhammad, we are not at liberty to conclude from this that he was inspired to declare the truth about things which we cannot verify. We are only at liberty to infer the excellence of his moral precepts, or of the means which he devised for so working upon men as to get them obeyed, or of the social and political machinery which he set up. And it would require a great amount of careful examination into the history of those nations to determine which of these things had the greater share in the result. So that here again it is the Prophet's knowledge of human nature, and his sympathy with it, that are verified; not his divine inspiration, or his knowledge of theology.

If there were only one Prophet, indeed, it might well seem a difficult and even an ungracious task to decide upon what points we would trust him, and on what we would doubt his authority; seeing what help and furtherance all men have gained in all ages from those who saw more clearly, who felt more strongly, and who sought the truth with more single heart than their weaker brethren. But there is not only one Prophet; and while the consent of many upon that which, as men, they had real means of knowing and did know, has endured to the end, and been honourably built into the great fabric of human knowledge, the diverse witness of some about that which they did not and could not know remains as a warning to us that to exaggerate the prophetic authority is to misuse it, and to dishonour those who have sought only to help and further us after their power. It is hardly in human nature that a man should quite accurately gauge the limits of his own insight; but it is the duty of those who profit by his work to consider carefully where he may have been carried beyond it. If we must needs embalm his possible errors along with his solid achievements, and use his authority as an excuse for believing what he cannot have known, we make of his goodness an occasion to sin.

To consider only one other such witness: the followers of the Buddha have at least as much right to appeal to individual and social experience in support of the authority of the Eastern saviour. The special mark of his religion, it is said, that in which it has never been surpassed, is the comfort and consolation which it gives to the sick and sorrowful, the tender sympathy with which it soothes and assuages all the natural grief of men. And surely no triumph of social morality can be greater or nobler than that which has kept nearly half the human race from persecuting in the name of religion. If we are to trust the accounts of his early followers, he believed himself to have come upon earth with a divine and cosmic mission to set rolling the wheel of the law. Being a prince, he divested himself of his kingdom, and of his free will became acquainted with misery, that he might learn how to meet and subdue it. Could such a man speak falsely about solemn things? And as for his knowledge, was he not a man miraculous with powers more than man's? He was born of woman without the help of man; he rose into the air and was transfigured before his kinsmen; at last he went up bodily into heaven from the top of Adam's Peak. Is not his word to be believed in when he testifies of heavenly things?

If there were only he, and no other, with such claims! But there is Muhammad with his testimony; we cannot choose but listen to them both. The Prophet tells us that there is one God, and that we shall live forever in joy or misery, according as we believe in the Prophet or not. The Buddha says that there is no God, and that we shall be annihilated by and by if we are good enough. Both cannot be infallibly inspired; one or the other must have been the victim of a delusion, and thought he knew that which he really did not know. Who shall dare to say which? and how can we justify ourselves in believing that the other was not also deluded?

We are led, then, to these judgements following. The goodness and greatness of a man do not justify us in accepting a belief upon the warrant of his authority, unless there are reasonable grounds for supposing that he knew the truth of what he was saying. And there can be no grounds for supposing that a man knows that which we, without ceasing to be men, could not be supposed to verify.

If a chemist tells me, who am no chemist, that a certain substance can be made by putting together other substances in certain proportions and subjecting them to a known process, I am quite justified in believing this upon his authority, unless I know anything against his character or his judgement. For his professional training is one which tends to encourage veracity and the honest pursuit of truth, and to produce a dislike of hasty conclusions and slovenly investigation. And I have reasonable ground for supposing that he knows the truth of what he is saying, for although I am no chemist, I can be made to understand so much of the methods and processes of the science as makes it conceivable to me that, without ceasing to be man, I might verify the statement. I may never actually verify it, or even see any experiment which goes toward verifying it; but still I have quite reason enough to justify me in believing that the verification is within the reach of human appliances and powers, and in particular that it has been actually performed by my informant. His result, the belief to which he has been led by his enquiries, is valid not only for himself but for others; it is watched and tested by those who are working in the same ground and who know that no greater service can be rendered to science than the purification of accepted results from the errors which may have crept into them. It is in this way that the result becomes common property, a right object of belief, which is a social affair and matter of public business. Thus it is to be observed that his authority is valid because there are those who question it and verify it; that it is precisely this process of examining and purifying that keeps alive among investigators the love of that which shall stand all possible tests, the sense of public responsibility as of those whose work, if well done, shall remain as the enduring heritage of mankind.

But if my chemist tells me that an atom of oxygen has existed unaltered in weight and rate of vibration throughout all time, I have no right to believe this on his authority, for it is a thing which he cannot know without ceasing to be man. He may quite honestly believe that this statement is a fair inference from his experiments, but in that case his judgement is at fault. A very simple consideration of the character of experiments would show him that they never can lead to results of such a kind; that being themselves only approximate and limited, they cannot give us knowledge which is exact and universal. No eminence of character and genius can give a man authority enough to justify us in believing him when he makes statements implying exact or universal knowledge.

Again, an Arctic explorer may tell us that in a given latitude and longitude he has experienced such and such a degree of cold, that the sea was of such a depth, and the ice of such a character. We should be quite right to believe him, in the absence of any stain upon his veracity. It is conceivable that we might, without ceasing to be men, go there and verify his statement; it can be tested by the witness of his companions, and there is adequate ground for supposing that he knows the truth of what he is saying. But if an old whaler tells us that the ice is three hundred feet thick all the way up to the Pole, we shall not be justified in believing him. For although the statement may be capable of verification by man, it is certainly not capable of verification by *him*, with any means and appliances which he has possessed; and he must have persuaded himself of the truth of it by some means which does not attach any credit to his testimony. Even if, therefore, the matter affirmed is within the reach of human knowledge, we have no right to accept it upon authority unless it is within the reach of our informant's knowledge.

What shall we say of that authority, more venerable and august than any individual witness, the time-honoured tradition of the human race? An atmosphere of beliefs and conceptions has been formed by the labours and struggles of our forefathers, which enables us to breathe amid the various and complex circumstances of our life. It is around and about us and within us; we cannot think except in the forms and processes of thought which it supplies. Is it possible to doubt and to test it? and if possible, is it right?

We shall find reason to answer that it is not only possible and right, but our bounden duty; that the main purpose of the tradition itself is to supply us with the means of asking questions, of testing and inquiring into things; that if we misuse it, and take it as a collection of cut-and-dried statements, to be accepted without further enquiry, we are not only injuring ourselves here, but by refusing to do our part toward the building up of the fabric which shall be inherited by our children, we are tending to cut off ourselves and our race from the human line.

Let us first take care to distinguish a kind of tradition which especially requires to be examined and called in question, because it especially shrinks from enquiry. Suppose that a medicine man in Central Africa tells his tribe that a certain powerful medicine in his tent will be propitiated if they kill their cattle; and that the tribe believe him. Whether the medicine was propitiated or not, there are no means of verifying, but the cattle are gone. Still the belief may be kept up in the tribe that propitiation has been effected in this way; and in a later generation it will be all the easier for another medicine man to persuade them to a similar act. Here the only reason for belief is that everybody has believed the thing for so long that it must be true. And yet the belief was founded on fraud, and has been propagated by credulity. That man will undoubtedly do right, and be a friend of men who shall call it in question and see that there is no evidence for it, help his neighbours to see as he does, and even, if need be, go into the holy tent and break the medicine.

The rule, which should guide us in such cases is simple and obvious enough: that the aggregate testimony of our neighbours is subject to the same conditions as the testimony of anyone of them. Namely, we have no right to believe a thing true because everybody says so, unless there are good grounds for believing that some one person at least has the means of knowing what is true, and is speaking the truth so far as he knows it. However many nations and generations of men are brought into the witness box, they cannot testify to anything which they do not know. Every man who has accepted the statement from somebody else, without himself testing and verifying it, is out of court; his word is worth nothing at all. And when we get back at last to the true birth and beginning of the statement, two serious questions must be disposed of in regard to him who first made it: was he mistaken in thinking that he *knew* about this matter, or was he lying?

This last question is unfortunately a very actual and practical one even to us at this day and in this country. We have no occasion to go to La Salette,[48] or to Central Africa, or to Lourdes,[49] for examples of

---

48 [La Salette-Fallavaux is a village in south-east France. Our Lady of La Salette was an apparition of the Virgin Mary reported by two children in 1846.]

49 [A small town in south-west France. Our Lady of Lourdes was an apparition of the Virgin Mary reported by a girl in 1858.]

immoral and debasing superstition. It is only too possible for a child to grow up in London surrounded by an atmosphere of beliefs fit only for the savage, which have in our own time been founded in fraud and propagated by credulity.

Laying aside, then, such tradition as is handed on without testing by successive generations, let us consider that which is truly built up out of the common experience of mankind. This great fabric is for the guidance of our thoughts, and through them of our actions, both in the moral and in the material world. In the moral world, for example, it gives us the conceptions of right in general, of justice, of truth, of beneficence, and the like. These are given as conceptions, not as statements or propositions; they answer to certain definite instincts, which are certainly within us, however they came there. That it is right to be beneficent is matter of immediate personal experience; for when a man retires within himself and there finds something, wider and more lasting than his solitary personality which says, 'I want to do right,' as well as, 'I want to do good to man,' he can verify by direct observation that one instinct is founded upon and agrees fully with the other. And it is his duty so to verify this and all similar statements.

The tradition says also, at a definite place and time, that such and such actions are just, or true, or beneficent. For all such rules a further enquiry is necessary, since they are sometimes established by an authority other than that of the moral sense founded on experience. Until recently, the moral tradition of our own country—and indeed of all Europe—taught that it was beneficent to give money indiscriminately to beggars. But the questioning of this rule, and investigation into it, led men to see that true beneficence is that which helps a man to do the work which he is most fitted for, not that which keeps and encourages him in idleness; and that to neglect this distinction in the present is to prepare pauperism and misery for the future. By this testing and discussion, not only has practice been purified and made more beneficent, but the very conception of beneficence has been made wider and wiser. Now here the great social heirloom consists of two parts: the instinct of beneficence, which makes a certain side of our nature, when predominant, wish to do good to men; and the intellectual conception of beneficence, which we can compare with any proposed course of conduct and ask, 'Is this beneficent or not?' By the continual asking and answering of such questions the conception grows in breadth and distinctness, and the instinct becomes strengthened and purified. It appears then that the great use of the conception, the intellectual part of the heirloom, is to enable us to ask questions; that it grows and is kept straight by means of these questions; and if we do not use it for that purpose we shall gradually lose it altogether, and be left with a mere code of regulations which cannot rightly be called morality at all.

Such considerations apply even more obviously and clearly, if possible, to the store of beliefs and conceptions which our fathers have amassed for us in respect of the material world. We are ready to laugh at the rule of thumb of the Australian, who continues to tie his hatchet to the side of the handle, although the Birmingham fitter has made a hole on purpose for him to put the handle in. His people have tied up hatchets so for ages: who is he that he should set himself up against their wisdom? He has sunk so low that he cannot do what some of them must have done in the far distant past—call in question an established usage, and invent or learn something better. Yet here, in the dim beginning of knowledge, where science and art are one, we find only the same simple rule which applies to the highest and deepest growths of that cosmic Tree; to its loftiest flower-tipped branches as well as to the profoundest of its hidden roots; the rule, namely, that what is stored up and handed down to us is rightly used by those who act as the makers acted, when they stored it up; those who use it to ask further questions, to examine, to investigate; who try honestly and solemnly to find out what is the right way of looking at things and of dealing with them.

A question rightly asked is already half answered, said Jacobi;[50] we may add that the method of solution is the other half of the answer, and that the actual result counts for nothing by the side of these two. For an example let us go to the telegraph, where theory and practice, grown each to years of discretion, are marvellously wedded for the fruitful service of men. Ohm[51] found that the strength of an electric current is directly proportional to the strength of the battery which produces it, and inversely as the length of the wire along which it has to travel. This is called Ohm's law; but the result, regarded as a statement to be believed, is not the valuable part of it. The first half is the question: what relation holds good between these quantities? So put, the question involves already the conception of strength of current, and of strength of battery, as quantities to be measured and compared; it hints clearly

50 [Friedrich Heinrich Jacobi (1743–1819) was a German philosopher and literarist. He popularized the term nihilism, which argues that life is without objective meaning, purpose or intrinsic value.]
51 [Georg Simon Ohm (1789–1854) was a German physicist and mathematician. The unit of electrical resistance is named after him.]

that these are the things to be attended to in the study of electric currents. The second half is the method of investigation; how to measure these quantities, what instruments are required for the experiment, and how are they to be used? The student who begins to learn about electricity is not asked to believe in Ohm's law: he is made to understand the question, he is placed before the apparatus, and he is taught to verify it. He learns to do things, not to think he knows things; to use instruments and to ask questions, not to accept a traditional statement. The question which required a genius to ask it rightly is answered by a tyro.[52] If Ohm's law were suddenly lost and forgotten by all men, while the question and the method of solution remained, the result could be rediscovered in an hour. But the result by itself, if known to a people who could not comprehend the value of the question or the means of solving it, would be like a watch in the hands of a savage who could not wind it up, or an iron steam-ship worked by Spanish engineers.

In regard, then, to the sacred tradition of humanity, we learn that it consists, not in propositions or statements which are to be accepted and believed on the authority of the tradition, but in questions rightly asked, in conceptions which enable us to ask further questions, and in methods of answering questions. The value of all these things depends on their being tested day by day. The very sacredness of the precious deposit imposes upon us the duty and the responsibility of testing it, of purifying and enlarging it to the utmost of our power. He who makes use of its results to stifle his own doubts, or to hamper the enquiry of others, is guilty of a sacrilege which centuries shall never be able to blot out. When the labours and questionings of honest and brave men shall have built up the fabric of known truth to a glory which we in this generation can neither hope for nor imagine, in that pure and holy temple he shall have no part nor lot, but his name and his works shall be cast out into the darkness of oblivion forever.

III. The Limits of Inference

The question in what cases we may believe that which goes beyond our experience, is a very large and delicate one, extending to the whole range of scientific method, and requiring a considerable increase in the application of it before it can be answered with anything approaching to completeness. But one rule, lying on the threshold of the subject, of

---

52 [A beginner or a novice.]

extreme simplicity and vast practical importance, may here be touched upon and shortly laid down.

A little reflection will show us that every belief, even the simplest and most fundamental, goes beyond experience when regarded as a guide to our actions. A burnt child dreads the fire, because it believes that the fire will burn it today just as it did yesterday; but this belief goes beyond experience, and assumes that the unknown fire of today is like the known fire of yesterday. Even the belief that the child was burnt yesterday goes beyond *present* experience, which contains only the memory of a burning, and not the burning itself; it assumes, therefore, that this memory is trustworthy, although we know that a memory may often be mistaken. But if it is to be used as a guide to action, as a hint of what the future is to be, it must assume something about that future, namely, that it will be consistent with the supposition that the burning really took place yesterday; which is going beyond experience. Even the fundamental 'I am,' which cannot be doubted, is no guide to action until it takes to itself 'I shall be,' which goes beyond experience. The question is not, therefore, 'May we believe what goes beyond experience?' for this is involved in the very nature of belief; but 'How far and in what manner may we add to our experience in forming our beliefs?'

And an answer, of utter simplicity and universality, is suggested by the example we have taken: a burnt child dreads the fire. We may go beyond experience by assuming that what we do not know is like what we do know; or, in other words, we may add to our experience on the assumption of a uniformity in nature. What this uniformity precisely is, how we grow in the knowledge of it from generation to generation, these are questions which for the present we lay aside, being content to examine two instances which may serve to make plainer the nature of the rule.

From certain observations made with the spectroscope, we infer the existence of hydrogen in the sun. By looking into the spectroscope when the sun is shining on its slit, we see certain definite bright lines: and experiments made upon bodies on the earth have taught us that when these bright lines are seen hydrogen is the source of them. We assume, then, that the unknown bright lines in the sun are like the known bright lines of the laboratory, and that hydrogen in the sun behaves as hydrogen under similar circumstances would behave on the earth.

But are we not trusting our spectroscope too much? Surely, having found it to be trustworthy for terrestrial substances, where its statements can be verified by man, we are justified in accepting its testimony in other like cases; but not when it gives us information about things in the sun, where its testimony cannot be directly verified by man?

Certainly, we want to know a little more before this inference can be justified; and fortunately we do know this. The spectroscope testifies to exactly the same thing in the two cases; namely, that light-vibrations of a certain rate are being sent through it. Its construction is such that if it were wrong about this in one case, it would be wrong in the other. When we come to look into the matter, we find that we have really assumed the matter of the sun to be like the matter of the earth, made up of a certain number of distinct substances; and that each of these, when very hot, has a distinct rate of vibration, by which it may be recognized and singled out from the rest. But this is the kind of assumption which we are justified in using when we add to our experience. It is an assumption of uniformity in nature, and can only be checked by comparison with many similar assumptions which we have to make in other such cases.

But is this a true belief, of the existence of hydrogen in the sun? Can it help in the right guidance of human action?

Certainly not, if it is accepted on unworthy grounds, and without some understanding of the process by which it is got at. But when this process is taken in as the ground of the belief, it becomes a very serious and practical matter. For if there is no hydrogen in the sun, the spectroscope—that is to say, the measurement of rates of vibration—must be an uncertain guide in recognizing different substances; and consequently it ought not to be used in chemical analysis—in assaying, for example—to the great saving of time, trouble, and money. Whereas the acceptance of the spectroscopic method as trustworthy, has enriched us not only with new metals, which is a great thing, but with new processes of investigation, which is vastly greater.

For another example, let us consider the way in which we infer the truth of an historical event—say the siege of Syracuse in the Peloponnesian War.[53] Our experience is that manuscripts exist which are said to be and which call themselves manuscripts of the history of Thucydides;[54] that in other manuscripts, stated to be by later historians, he is described as living during the time of the war; and that

---

53 [The Peloponnesian War (BC 431–404) was fought by Athens and its empire against the Peloponnesian League led by Sparta.]

54 [Thucydides (BC 460–400) was an Athenian historian and general. His *History of the Peloponnesian War* describes the Peloponnesian War.]

books, supposed to date from the revival of learning, tell us how these manuscripts had been preserved and were then acquired. We find also that men do not, as a rule, forge books and histories without a special motive; we assume that in this respect men in the past were like men in the present; and we observe that in this case no special motive was present. That is, we add to our experience on the assumption of a uniformity in the characters of men. Because our knowledge of this uniformity is far less complete and exact than our knowledge of that which obtains in physics, inferences of the historical kind are more precarious and less exact than inferences in many other sciences.

But if there is any special reason to suspect the character of the persons who wrote or transmitted certain books, the case becomes altered. If a group of documents give internal evidence that they were produced among people who forged books in the names of others, and who, in describing events, suppressed those things which did not suit them, while they amplified such as did suit them; who not only committed these crimes, but gloried in them as proofs of humility and zeal; then we must say that upon such documents no true historical inference can be founded, but only unsatisfactory conjecture.

We may, then, add to our experience on the assumption of a uniformity in nature; we may fill in our picture of what is and has been, as experience gives it us, in such a way as to make the whole consistent with this uniformity. And practically demonstrative inference—that which gives us a right to believe in the result of it—is a clear showing that in no other way than by the truth of this result can the uniformity of nature be saved.

No evidence, therefore, can justify us in believing the truth of a statement which is contrary to, or outside of, the uniformity of nature. If our experience is such that it cannot be filled up consistently with uniformity, all we have a right to conclude is that there is something wrong somewhere; but the possibility of inference is taken away; we must rest in our experience, and not go beyond it at all. If an event really happened which was not a part of the uniformity of nature, it would have two properties: no evidence could give the right to believe it to any except those whose actual experience it was; and no inference worthy of belief could be founded upon it at all.

Are we then bound to believe that nature is absolutely and universally uniform? Certainly not; we have no right to believe anything of this kind. The rule only tells us that in forming beliefs which go beyond our experience, we may make the assumption that nature is practically uniform so far as we are concerned. Within the range of human action and verification, we may form, by help of this assumption, actual beliefs; beyond it, only those hypotheses which serve for the more accurate asking of questions.

To sum up:

We may believe what goes beyond our experience, only when it is inferred from that experience by the assumption that what we do not know is like what we know.

We may believe the statement of another person, when there is reasonable ground for supposing that he knows the matter of which he speaks, and that he is speaking the truth so far as he knows it.

It is wrong in all cases to believe on insufficient evidence; and where it is presumption to doubt and to investigate, there it is worse than presumption to believe.

4. The Ethics of Religion

THE WORD *RELIGION* IS used in many different meanings, and there have been not a few controversies in which the main difference between the contending parties was only this, that they understood by *religion* two different things. I will therefore begin by setting forth as clearly as I can one or two of the meanings which the word appears to have in popular speech.

First, then, it may mean a body of doctrines, as in the common phrase, 'The truth of the Christian religion;' or in this sentence, 'The religion of the Buddha teaches that the soul is not a distinct substance.' Opinions differ upon the question what doctrines may properly be called religious; some people holding that there can be no religion without belief in a God and in a future life, so that in their judgement the body of doctrines must necessarily include these two; while others would insist upon other special dogmas being included, before they could consent to call the system by this name. But the number of such people is daily diminishing, by reason of the spread and the increase of our knowledge about distant countries and races. To me, indeed, it would seem rash to assert of any doctrine or its contrary that it might not form part of a religion. But, fortunately, it is not necessary to any part of the discussion on which I propose to enter that this question should be settled.

Secondly, religion may mean a *ceremonial* or *cult*, involving an organized priesthood and a machinery of sacred things and places. In this sense we speak of the clergy as ministers of religion, or of a state as tolerating the practice of certain religions. There is a somewhat wider meaning which it will be convenient to consider together with this one, and as a mere extension of it, namely, that in which religion stands for the influence of a certain priesthood. A religion is sometimes said to have been successful when it has got its priests into power; thus some writers speak of the wonderfully rapid success of Christianity. A nation is said to have embraced a religion when the authorities of that nation have granted privileges to the clergy, have made them as far as possible the leaders of society, and have given them a considerable share in the management of public affairs. So the northern nations of Europe are said to have embraced the Catholic religion at an early date. The reason why it seems to me convenient to take these two meanings together is, that they are both related to the priesthood. Although the priesthood itself is not called religion, so far as I know, yet the word is used for the general influence and professional acts of the priesthood.

Thirdly, religion may mean a body of precepts or code of rules, intended to guide human conduct, as in this sentence of the authorized version of the New Testament: 'Pure religion and undefiled before God and the Father is this, to visit the fatherless and widows in their affliction, and to keep himself unspotted from the world' (James 1:27). It is sometimes difficult to draw the line between this meaning and the last, for it is a mark of the great majority of religions that they confound ceremonial observances with duties having real moral obligation. Thus in the Jewish decalogue the command to do no work on Saturdays is found side by side with the prohibition of murder and theft. It might seem to be the more correct as well as the more philosophical course to follow in this matter the distinction made by Butler[55] between *moral* and *positive* commands, and to class all those precepts which are not of universal moral obligation under the head of ceremonial. And, in fact, when we come to examine the matter from the point of view of morality, the distinction is of the utmost importance. But from the point of view of religion there are difficulties in making it. In the first place, the distinction is not made, or is not understood, by religious folk in general. Innumerable tracts and pretty stories impress upon us that Sabbath-breaking is rather worse than stealing, and leads naturally on to materialism and murder. Less than a hundred years ago sacrilege was punishable by burning in France, and murder by simple decapitation. In the next place, if we pick out a religion at haphazard, we shall find that it is not at all easy to divide its precepts into those which are really of moral obligation and those which are indifferent and of a ceremonial character. We may find precepts unconnected with any ceremonial, and yet positively immoral; and ceremonials may be immoral in themselves, or constructively immoral on account of their known symbolism. On the whole, it seems to me most convenient to draw the plain and obvious distinction between those actions which a religion prescribes to *all* its followers, whether the actions are ceremonial or not, and those which are prescribed only as professional actions of a sacerdotal class. The latter will come under what I have called the second meaning of religion, the professional acts and the influence of a priesthood. In the third meaning will be included all that practically

---

55 [Joseph Butler (1692–1752) was an English bishop, theologian, apologist and philosopher.]

guides the life of a layman, in so far as this guidance is supplied to him by his religion.

Fourthly, and lastly, there is a meaning of the word *religion* which has been coming more and more prominently forward of late years, till it has even threatened to supersede all the others. Religion has been defined as *morality touched with emotion.* I will not here adopt this definition, because I wish to deal with the concrete in the first place, and only to pass on to the abstract in so far as that previous study appears to lead to it. I wish to consider the facts of religion as we find them, and not ideal possibilities. 'Yes, but,' every one will say, 'if you mean my own religion, it is already, as a matter of fact, morality touched with emotion. It is the highest morality touched with the purest emotion, an emotion directed toward the most worthy of objects.' Unfortunately we do not mean your religion alone, but all manner of heresies and heathenisms along with it: the religions of the Thug, of the Jesuit, of the South Sea cannibal, of Confucius, of the poor Indian with his untutored mind, of the Peculiar People, of the Mormons, and of the old cat-worshiping Egyptian. It must be clear that we shall restrict ourselves to a very narrow circle of what are commonly called religious facts, unless we include in our considerations not only morality touched with emotion, but also immorality touched with emotion. In fact, what is really touched with emotion in any case is that body of precepts for the guidance of a layman's life which we have taken to be the third meaning of religion. In that collection of precepts there may be some agreeable to morality, and some repugnant to it, and some indifferent, but being all enjoined by the religion they will all be touched by the same religious emotion. Shall we then say that religion means a feeling, an emotion, an habitual attitude of mind toward some object or objects, or toward life in general, which has a bearing upon the way in which men regard the rules of conduct? I think the last phrase should be left out. An habitual attitude of mind, of a religious character, does always have some bearing upon the way in which men regard the rules of conduct; but it seems sometimes as if this were an accident, and not the essence of the religious feeling. Some devout people prefer to have their devotion pure and simple, without admixture of any such application—they do not want to listen to 'cauld morality.'[56] And it seems as if the religious feeling of the Greeks, and partly also of our own ances-

---

56 ['Cold morality' from the Scots. When applied to sermons it means a moral discourse devoid of Evangelical fervour.]

tors, was so far divorced from morality that it affected it only, as it were, by a side-wind, through the influence of the character and example of the Gods. So that it seems only likely to create confusion if we mix up morality with this fourth meaning of religion. Sometimes religion means a code of precepts, and sometimes it means a devotional habit of mind; the two things are sometimes connected, but also they are sometimes quite distinct. But that the connection of these two things is more and more insisted on, that it is the keynote of the apparent revival of religion which has taken place in this century, is a very significant fact, about which there is more to be said.

As to the nature of this devotional habit of mind, there are no doubt many who would like a closer definition. But I am not at all prepared to say what attitude of mind may properly be called religious, and what may not. Some will hold that religion must have a person for its object; but the Buddha was filled with religious feeling, and yet he had no personal object. Spinoza, the God-intoxicated man, had no personal object for his devotion. It might be possible to frame a definition which would fairly include all cases, but it would require the expenditure of vast ingenuity and research, and would not, I am inclined to think, be of much use when it was obtained.

Nor is the difficulty to be got over by taking any definite and well-organized sect, whose principles are settled in black and white; for example, the Roman Catholic Church, whose seamless unity has just been exhibited and protected by an Ecumenical Council. Shall we listen to Mr. Mivart,[57] who 'execrates without reserve Marian[58] persecutions, the Massacre of St. Bartholomew,[59] and all similar acts'? or to the editor of the *Dublin Review*, who thinks that a teacher of false doctrines 'should be visited by the law with just that amount of severity which the public sentiment will bear'? For assuredly common-sense morality will pass very different judgements on these two distinct religions, although it appears that experts have found room for both of them within the limits of the Vatican definitions.

---

57 [St George Jackson Mivart (1827–1900) was an English biologist. He was as ardent believer in Darwin's theory of natural selection but later became a fierce critic and attempted to reconcile Darwin's theory with the beliefs of the Catholic Church. He ended up by being condemned by both parties.]

58 [Relating to the Virgin Mary.]

59 [The St Bartholomew's Day Massacre of 1572 was Catholic mob murderous violence against Calvinist Protestants in France.]

Moreover, there is very great good to be got by widening our view of what may be contained in religion. If we go to a man and propose to test his own religion by the canons of common-sense morality, he will be, most likely, offended, for he will say that his religion is far too sublime and exalted to be affected by considerations of that sort. But he will have no such objection in the case of other people's religion. And when he has found that in the name of religion other people, in other circumstances, have believed in doctrines that were false, have supported priesthoods that were social evils, have taken wrong for right, and have even poisoned the very sources of morality, he may be tempted to ask himself, 'Is there no trace of any of these evils in my own religion, or at least in my own conception and practice of it?' And that is just what we want him to do. Bring your doctrines, your priesthoods, your precepts, yea, even the inner devotion of your soul, before the tribunal of conscience; she is no man's and no God's vicar, but the supreme judge of men and Gods.

Let us enquire, then, what morality has to say in regard to religious doctrines. It deals with the *manner* of religious belief directly, and with the *matter* indirectly. Religious beliefs must be founded on evidence; if they are not so founded, it is wrong to hold them. The rule of right conduct in this matter is exactly the opposite of that implied in the two famous texts: 'He that believeth not shall be damned,' and 'Blessed are they that have not seen and yet have believed.' For a man who clearly felt and recognized the duty of intellectual honesty, of carefully testing every belief before he received it, and especially before he recommended it to others, it would be impossible to ascribe the profoundly immoral teaching of these texts to a true prophet or worthy leader of humanity. It will comfort those who wish to preserve their reverence for the character of a great teacher to remember that one of these sayings is in the well-known forged passage at the end of the second gospel, and that the other occurs only in the late and legendary fourth gospel; both being described as spoken under utterly impossible circumstances. These precepts belong to the Church and not to the Gospel. But whoever wrote either of them down as a deliverance of one whom he supposed to be a divine teacher, has thereby written down himself as a man void of intellectual honesty, as a man whose word cannot be trusted, as a man who would accept and spread about any kind of baseless fiction for fear of believing too little.

So far as to the manner of religious belief. Let us now enquire what bearing morality has upon its matter. We may see at once that this can only be indirect; for the rightness or wrongness of belief in a doctrine depends only upon the nature of the evidence for it, and not upon what the doctrine is. But there is a very important way in which religious doctrine may lead to morality or immorality, and in which, therefore, morality has a bearing upon doctrine. It is when that doctrine declares the character and actions of the Gods who are regarded as objects of reverence and worship. If a God is represented as doing that which is clearly wrong, and is still held up to the reverence of men, they will be tempted to think that in doing this wrong thing they are not so very wrong after all, but are only following an example which all men respect. So says Plato:

> We must not tell a youthful listener that he will be doing nothing extraordinary if he commit the foulest crimes nor yet if he chastise the crimes of a father in the most unscrupulous manner, but will simply be doing what the first and greatest of the Gods have done before him. ...
>
> Nor yet is it proper to say in any case—what is indeed untrue—that Gods wage war against Gods, and intrigue and fight among themselves; that is, if the future guardians of our state are to deem it a most disgraceful thing to quarrel lightly with one another: far less ought we to select as subjects for fiction and embroidery the battles of the giants, and numerous other feuds of all sorts, in which Gods and heroes fight against their own kith and kin. But if there is any possibility of persuading them that to quarrel with one's fellow is a sin of which no member of a state was ever guilty, such ought rather to be the language held to our children from the first, by old men and old women, and all elderly persons; and such is the strain in which our poets must be compelled to write. But stories like the chaining of Hera by her son, and the flinging of Hephaistos out of heaven for trying to take his mother's part when his father was beating her, and all those battles of the Gods which are to be found in Homer, must be refused admittance into our state, whether they be allegorical or not. For a child cannot discriminate between what is allegory and what is not; and whatever at that age is adopted as a matter of belief has a tendency to become fixed and indelible, and therefore, perhaps, we ought to esteem it of the greatest importance that the fictions which children first hear should be adapted in the most perfect manner to the promotion of virtue.— (*Republic* ii. 378. Tr. Davies and Vaughan.)

And Seneca[60] says the same thing, with still more reason in his day and country: 'What else is this appeal to the precedent of the Gods

---

60 [Lucius Annaeus Seneca known as Seneca the Younger (BC 4 to 65 AD) was a Roman Stoic philosopher, statesman and dramatist.]

for, but to inflame our lusts, and to furnish license and excuse for the corrupt act under the divine protection?' And again, of the character of Jupiter as described in the popular legends: 'This has led to no other result than to deprive sin of its shame in man's eyes, by showing him the God no better than himself.' In Imperial Rome, the sink of all nations, it was not uncommon to find 'the intending sinner addressing to the deified vice which he contemplated a prayer for the success of his design; the adulteress imploring of Venus the favours of her paramour; ... the thief praying to Hermes Dolios for aid in his enterprise, or offering up to him the first fruits of his plunder; ... youths entreating Hercules to expedite the death of a rich uncle.'

When we reflect that criminal deities were worshiped all over the empire, we cannot but wonder that any good people were left; that man could still be holy, although every God was vile. Yet this was undoubtedly the case; the social forces worked steadily on wherever there was peace and a settled government and municipal freedom; and the wicked stories of theologians were somehow explained away and disregarded. If men were no better than their religions, the world would be a hell indeed.

It is very important, however, to consider what really ought to be done in the case of stories like these. When the poet sings that Zeus kicked Hephaistos out of heaven for trying to help his mother, Plato says that this fiction must be suppressed by law. We cannot follow him there, for since his time we have had too much of trying to suppress false doctrines by law. Plato thinks it quite obviously clear that God cannot produce evil, and he would stop everybody's mouth who ventured to say that he can. But in regard to the doctrine itself, we can only ask, 'Is it true?' And that is a question to be settled by evidence. Did Zeus commit this crime, or did he not? We must ask the apologists, the reconcilers of religion and science, what evidence they can produce to prove that Zeus kicked Hephaistos out of heaven. That a doctrine may lead to immoral consequences is no reason for disbelieving it. But whether the doctrine were true or false, one thing does clearly follow from its moral character: namely this, that if Zeus behaved as he is said to have behaved he ought not to be worshiped. To those who complain of his violence and injustice it is no answer to say that the divine attributes are far above human comprehension; that the ways of Zeus are not our ways, neither are his thoughts our thoughts. If he is to be worshiped, he must do something vaster and nobler and greater than good men do, but it must be like what they do in its goodness. His actions must not be merely a magnified copy of what bad men do. So soon as they are thus represented, morality has something to say. Not indeed about the fact; for it is not conscience, but reason, that has to judge matters of fact; but about the worship of a character so represented. If there really is good evidence that Zeus kicked Hephaistos out of heaven, and seduced Alkmene by a mean trick, say so by all means; but say also that it is wrong to salute his priests or to make offerings in his temple.

When men do their duty in this respect, morality has a very curious indirect effect on the religious doctrine itself. As soon as the offerings become less frequent, the evidence for the doctrine begins to fade away; the process of theological interpretation gradually brings out the true inner meaning of it, that Zeus did not kick Hephaistos out of heaven, and did not seduce Alkmene.

Is this a merely theoretical discussion about far-away things? Let us come back for a moment to our own time and country, and think whether there can be any lesson for us in this refusal of common-sense morality to worship a deity whose actions are a magnified copy of what bad men do. There are three doctrines which find very wide acceptance among our countrymen at the present day: the doctrines of original sin, of a vicarious sacrifice, and of eternal punishments. We are not concerned with any refined evaporations of these doctrines which are exhaled by courtly theologians, but with the naked statements which are put into the minds of children and of ignorant people, which are taught broadcast and without shame in denominational schools. Father Faber,[61] good soul, persuaded himself that after all only a very few people would be really damned, and Father Oxenham[62] gives one the impression that it will not hurt even them very much. But one learns the practical teaching of the Church from such books as *A Glimpse of Hell*, where a child is described as thrown between the bars upon the burning coals, there to writhe forever. The masses do not get the elegant emasculations of Father Faber and Father Oxenham; they get 'a Glimpse of Hell.'

Now to condemn all mankind for the sin of Adam and Eve; to let the innocent suffer for the guilty; to keep anyone alive in torture forever and ever; these actions are simply magnified copies of what bad men

---

61 [Frederick William Faber (1814–63) was an English hymn writer and theologian, who converted from Anglicanism to the Catholic priesthood.]

62 [Henry Nutcombe Oxenham (1829–88) was an English ecclesiologist, theologian, author and translator, who was ordained in the Church of England and later converted to the Roman Catholic faith.]

do. No juggling with 'divine justice and mercy' can make them anything else. This must be said to all kinds and conditions of men: that if God holds all mankind guilty for the sin of Adam, if he has visited upon the innocent the punishment of the guilty, if he is to torture any single soul forever, then it is wrong to worship him.

But there is something to be said also to those who think that religious beliefs are not indeed true, but are useful for the masses; who deprecate any open and public argument against them, and think that all sceptical books should be published at a high price; who go to church, not because they approve of it themselves, but to set an example to the servants. Let us ask them to ponder the words of Plato, who, like them, thought that all these tales of the Gods were fables, but still fables which might be useful to amuse children with: '*We ought to esteem it of the greatest importance that the fictions which children first hear should be adapted in the most perfect manner to the promotion of virtue.*' If we grant to you that it is good for poor people and children to believe some of these fictions, is it not better, at least, that they should believe those which are adapted to the promotion of virtue? Now the stories which you send your servants and children to hear are adapted to the promotion of vice. So far as the remedy is in your own hands, you are bound to apply it; stop your voluntary subscriptions and the moral support of your presence from any place where the criminal doctrines are taught. You will find more men and better men to preach that which is agreeable to their conscience, than to thunder out doctrines under which their minds are always uneasy, and which only a continual self-deception can keep them from feeling to be wicked.

Let us now go on to enquire what morality has to say in the matter of religious *ministrations*, the official acts and the general influence of a priesthood. This question seems to me a more difficult one than the former; at any rate it is not so easy to find general principles which are at once simple in their nature and clear to the conscience of any man who honestly considers them. One such principle, indeed, there is, which can hardly be stated in a Protestant country without meeting with a cordial response; being indeed that characteristic of our race which made the Reformation a necessity, and became the soul of the Protestant movement. I mean the principle which forbids the priest to come between a man and his conscience. If it be true, as our daily experience teaches us, that the moral sense gains in clearness and power by exercise, by the constant endeavour to find out and to see for ourselves what is right and what is wrong, it must be nothing short of a moral suicide to delegate our conscience to another man. It is true that when we are in difficulties and do not altogether see our way, we quite rightly seek counsel and advice of some friend who has more experience, more wisdom begot by it, more devotion to the right than ourselves, and who, not being involved in the difficulties which encompass us, may more easily see the way out of them. But such counsel does not and ought not to take the place of our private judgement; on the contrary, among wise men it is asked and given for the purpose of helping and supporting private judgement. I should go to my friend, not that he may tell me what to do, but that he may help me to see what is right.

Now, as we all know, there is a priesthood whose influence is not to be made light of, even in our own land, which claims to do two things: to declare with infallible authority what is right and what is wrong, and to take away the guilt of the sinner after confession has been made to it. The second of these claims we shall come back upon in connection with another part of the subject. But that claim is one which, as it seems to me, ought to condemn the priesthood making it in the eyes of every conscientious man. We must take care to keep this question to itself, and not to let it be confused with quite different ones. The priesthood in question, as we all know, has taught that as right which is not right, and has condemned as wrong some of the holiest duties of mankind. But this is not what we are here concerned with. Let us put an ideal case of a priesthood which, as a matter of fact, taught a morality agreeing with the healthy conscience of all men at a given time; but which, nevertheless, taught this as an infallible revelation. The tendency of such teaching, if really accepted, would be to destroy morality altogether, for it is of the very essence of the moral sense that it is a common perception by men of what is good for man. It arises, not in one man's mind by a flash of genius or a transport of ecstasy, but in all men's minds, as the fruit of their necessary intercourse and united labour for a common object. When an infallible authority is set up, the voice of this natural human conscience must be hushed and schooled, and made to speak the words of a formula. Obedience becomes the whole duty of man; and the notion of right is attached to a lifeless code of rules, instead of being the informing character of a nation. The natural consequence is that it fades gradually out and ends by disappearing altogether. I am not describing a purely conjectural state of things, but an effect which has actually been produced at various times and in considerable populations by the influence of the Catholic Church. It is true that we cannot find an actually crucial instance of a pure morality taught as an infallible revelation, and so in time ceasing to be morality for that reason alone. There are two circumstances which prevent this. One is that the

Catholic priesthood has always practically taught an imperfect morality, and that it is difficult to distinguish between the effects of precepts which are wrong in themselves, and precepts which are only wrong because of the manner in which they are enforced. The other circumstance is that the priesthood has very rarely found a population willing to place itself completely and absolutely under priestly control. Men must live together and work for common objects even in priest-ridden countries; and those conditions which in the course of ages have been able to create the moral sense cannot fail in some degree to recall it to men's minds and gradually to re-enforce it. Thus it comes about that a great and increasing portion of life breaks free from priestly influences, and is governed upon right and rational grounds. The goodness of men shows itself in time more powerful than the wickedness of some of their religions.

The practical inference is, then, that we ought to do all in our power to restrain and diminish the influence of any priesthood which claims to rule consciences. But when we attempt to go beyond this plain Protestant principle, we find that the question is one of history and politics. The question which we want to ask ourselves—'Is it right to support this or that priesthood?'—can only be answered by this other question, 'What has it done or got done?'

In asking this question, we must bear in mind that the word *priesthood*, as we have used it hitherto, has a very wide meaning—namely, it means any body of men who perform special ceremonies in the name of religion; a *ceremony* being an act which is prescribed by religion to that body of men, but not on account of its intrinsic rightness or wrongness. It includes, therefore, not only the priests of Catholicism, or of the Obi rites, who lay claim to a magical character and powers, but the more familiar clergymen or ministers of Protestant denominations, and the members of monastic orders. But there is a considerable difference, pointed out by Hume, between a priest who lays claim to a magical character and powers, and a clergymen, in the English sense, as it was understood in Hume's day, whose office was to remind people of their duties every Sunday, and to represent a certain standard of culture in remote country districts. It will, perhaps, conduce to clearness if we use the word *priest* exclusively in the first sense.

There is another confusion which we must endeavour to avoid, if we would really get at the truth of this matter. When one ventures to doubt whether the Catholic clergy has really been an unmixed blessing to Europe, one is generally met by the reply, 'You cannot find any fault with the Sermon on the Mount.' Now it would be too much to say that this has nothing to do with the question we were proposing to ask, for there is a sense in which the Sermon on the Mount and the Catholic clergy have something to do with each other. The Sermon on the Mount is admitted on all hands to be the best and most precious thing that Christianity has offered to the world; and it cannot be doubted that the Catholic clergy of East and West were the only spokesmen of Christianity until the Reformation, and are the spokesmen of the vast majority of Christians at this moment. But it must surely be unnecessary to say in a Protestant country that the Catholic Church and the Gospel are two very different things. The moral teaching of Christ, as partly preserved in the three first gospels, or—which is the same thing—the moral teaching of the great Rabbi Hillel, as partly preserved in the Pirkei Aboth,[63] is the expression of the conscience of a people who had fought long and heroically for their national existence. In that terrible conflict they had learned the supreme and overwhelming importance of conduct, the necessity for those who would survive of fighting manfully for their lives and making a stand against the hostile powers around; the weakness and uselessness of solitary and selfish efforts, the necessity for a man who would be a man to lose his poor single personality in the being of a greater and nobler combatant—the nation. And they said all this, after their fashion of short and potent sayings, perhaps better than any other men have said it before or since. 'If I am not for myself,' said the great Hillel, 'who is for me? And if I am only for myself, where is the use of me? *And if not now, when?*' It would be hard to find a more striking contrast than exists between the sturdy unselfish independence of this saying, and the abject and selfish servility of the priest-ridden claimant of the skies. It was this heroic people that produced the morality of the Sermon on the Mount. But it was not they who produced the priests and the dogmas of Catholicism. Shaven crowns, linen vestments, and the claim to priestly rule over consciences, these were dwellers on the banks of the Nile. The gospel indeed came out of Judaea, but the Church and her dogmas came out of Egypt. Not, as it is written, 'Out of Egypt have I called my son,' but 'Out of Egypt have I called my daughter.' St Gregory of Nazianzus[64] remarked with wonder that Egypt, having so lately worshiped bulls, goats, and crocodiles, was now teaching the world the worship of the

---

63 ['Chapters of our Fathers' is a collection of Jewish ethical teachings and maxims.]
64 [Gregory of Nazianzus (329–90) was an Archbishop of Constantinople and theologian.]

Trinity in its truest form. Poor, simple St Gregory! it was not that Egypt had risen higher, but that the world had sunk lower. The empire, which in the time of Augustus[65] had dreaded, and with reason, the corrupting influence of Egyptian superstitions, was now eaten up by them, and rapidly rotting away.

Then, when we ask what has been the influence of the Catholic clergy upon European nations, we are not inquiring about the results of accepting the morality of the Sermon on the Mount; we are inquiring into the effect of attaching an Egyptian priesthood, which teaches Egyptian dogmas, to the life and sayings of a Jewish prophet.

In this enquiry, which requires the knowledge of facts beyond our own immediate experience, we must make use of the great principle of authority, which enables us to profit by the experience of other men. The great civilized countries on the continent of Europe at the present day—France, Germany, Austria, and Italy—have had an extensive experience of the Catholic clergy for a great number of centuries, and they are forced by strong practical reasons to form a judgement upon the character and tendencies of an institution which is sufficiently powerful to command the attention of all who are interested in public affairs. We might add the experience of our forefathers three centuries ago, and of Ireland at this moment; but home politics are apt to be looked upon with other eyes than those of reason. Let us hear, then, the judgement of the civilized people of Europe on this question.

It is a matter of notoriety that an aider and abettor of clerical pretensions is regarded in France as an enemy of France and of Frenchmen; in Germany as an enemy of Germany and of Germans; in Austria as an enemy of Austria and Hungary, of both Austrians and Magyars; and in Italy as an enemy of Italy and the Italians. He is so regarded, not by a few wild and revolutionary enthusiasts who have cast away all the beliefs of their childhood and all bonds connecting them with the past, but by a great and increasing majority of sober and conscientious men of all creeds and persuasions, who are filled with a love for their country, and whose hopes and aims for the future are animated and guided by the examples of those who have gone before them, and by a sense of the continuity of national life. The profound conviction and determination of the people in all these countries, that the clergy must be restricted to a purely ceremonial province, and must not be

---

65 [Augustus (BC 63 to 14 AD) was considered the first Roman emperor, controlling the Roman Empire from BC 27 until his death in 14 AD.]

allowed to interfere, as clergy, in public affairs—this conviction and determination, I say, are not the effect of a rejection of the Catholic dogmas. Such rejection has not in fact been made in Catholic countries by the great majority. It involves many difficult speculative questions, the profound disturbance of old habits of thought, and the toilsome consideration of abstract ideas. But such is the happy inconsistency of human nature, that men who would be shocked and pained by a doubt about the central doctrines of their religions are far more really and practically shocked and pained by the moral consequences of clerical ascendency. About the dogmas they do not know; they were taught them in childhood, and have not enquired into them since, and therefore they are not competent witnesses to the truth of them. But about the priesthood they do know, by daily and hourly experience; and to its character they are competent witnesses. No man can express his convictions more forcibly than by acting upon them in a great and solemn matter of national importance. In all these countries the conviction of the serious and sober majority of the people is embodied, and is being daily embodied, in special legislation, openly and avowedly intended to guard against clerical aggression. The more closely the legislature of these countries reflects the popular will, the more clear and pronounced does this tendency become. It may be thwarted or evaded for the moment by constitutional devices and parliamentary tricks, but sooner or later the nation will be thoroughly represented in all of them: and as to what is then to be expected, let the panic of the clerical parties make answer.

This is a state of opinion and of feeling which we in our own country find it hard to understand, although it is one of the most persistent characters of our nation in past times. We have spoken so plainly and struck so hard in the past, that we seem to have won the right to let this matter alone. We think our enemies are dead, and we forget that our neighbour's enemies are plainly alive: and then we wonder that he does not sit down and be quiet as we are. We are not much accustomed to be afraid, and we never know when we are beaten. But those who are nearer to the danger feel a very real and, it seems to me, well-grounded fear. The whole structure of modern society, the fruit of long and painful efforts, the hopes of further improvement, the triumphs of justice, of freedom, and of light, the bonds of patriotism which make each nation one, the bonds of humanity which bring different nations together—all these they see to be menaced with a great and real and even pressing danger. For myself I confess that I cannot help feeling as they feel. It seems to me quite possible that the moral and intellectual culture of Europe, the light and the right, what makes life worth having and men worthy to have it, may be clean swept away by a revival of superstition. We are, perhaps, ourselves not free from such a domestic danger; but no one can doubt that the danger would speedily arise if all Europe at our side should become again barbaric, not with the weakness and docility of a barbarism which has never known better, but with the strength of a past civilization perverted to the service of evil.

Those who know best, then, about the Catholic priesthood at present, regard it as a standing menace to the state and to the moral fabric of society.

Some would have us believe that this condition of things is quite new, and has in fact been created by the Vatican Council. In the Middle Ages, they say, the Church did incalculable service; or even if you do not allow that, yet the ancient Egyptian priesthood invented many useful arts; or if you have read anything which is not to their credit, there were the Babylonians and Assyrians who had priests, thousands of years ago; and in fact, the more you go back into prehistoric ages, and the further you go away into distant countries, the less you can find to say against the priesthoods of those times and places. This statement, for which there is certainly much foundation, may be put into another form: the more you come forward into modern times and neighbouring countries, where the facts can actually be got at, the more complete is the evidence against the priesthoods of these times and places. But the whole argument is founded upon what is at least a doubtful view of human nature and of society. Just as an early school of geologists were accustomed to explain the present state of the earth's surface by supposing that in primitive ages the processes of geologic change were far more violent and rapid than they are now—so catastrophic, indeed, as to constitute a thoroughly different state of things—so there is a school of historians who think that the intimate structure of human nature, its capabilities of learning and of adapting itself to society, have so far altered within the historic period as to make the present processes of social change totally different in character from those even of the moderately distant past. They think that institutions and conditions which are plainly harmful to us now have at other times and places done good and serviceable work. War, pestilence, priestcraft, and slavery have been represented as positive boons to an early state of society. They are not blessings to us, it is true; but then times have altered very much.

On the other hand, a later school of geologists have seen reason to think that the processes of change have never, since the earth finally solidified, been very different from what they are now. More rapid, indeed, they must have been in early times, for many reasons; but not so very much more rapid as to constitute an entirely different state of things. And it does seem to me in like manner that a wider and more rational view of history will recognize more and more of the permanent, and less and less of the changeable, element in human nature. No doubt our ancestors of a thousand generations back were very different beings from ourselves; perhaps fifty thousand generations back they were not men at all. But the historic period is hardly to be stretched beyond two hundred generations; and it seems unreasonable to expect that in such a tiny page of our biography we can trace with clearness the growth and progress of a long life. Compare Egypt in the time of King Menes,[66] say six thousand years ago, with Spain in this present century, before Englishmen made any railways there: I suppose the main difference is that the Egyptians washed themselves. It seems more analogous to what we find in other fields of enquiry to suppose that there are certain great broad principles of human life which have been true all along; that certain conditions have always been favourable to the health of society, and certain other conditions always hurtful.

Now, although I have many times asked for it from those who said that somewhere and at some time mankind had derived benefits from a priesthood laying claim to a magical character and powers, I have never been able to get any evidence for their statement. Nobody will give me a date, and a latitude and longitude, that I may examine into the matter. 'In the Middle Ages the priests and monks were the sole depositaries of learning.' Quite so; a man burns your house to the ground, builds a wretched hovel on the ruins, and then takes credit for whatever shelter there is about the place. In the Middle Ages nearly all learned men were obliged to become priests and monks. 'Then again, the bishops have sometimes acted as tribunes of the people, to protect them against the tyranny of kings.' No doubt, when Pope and Caesar fall out, honest men may come by their own. If two men rob you in a dark lane, and then quarrel over the plunder, so that you get a chance to escape with your life, you will of course be very grateful to each of them for having prevented the other from killing you; but you would be much more grateful to a policeman who locked them both up. Two powers have sought to enslave the people, and have quarrelled with each other; certainly we are very much obliged to them for quarrelling,

---

66 [Menes is thought to have united Upper and Lower Egypt.]

but a condition of still greater happiness and security would be the non-existence of both.

I can find no evidence that seriously militates against the rule that the priest is at all times and in all places the enemy of all men—*Sacerdos semper, ubique, et omnibus inimicus.*[67] I do not deny that the priest is very often a most earnest and conscientious man, doing the very best that he knows of as well as he can do it. Lord Amberley[68] is quite right in saying that the blame rests more with the laity than with the priest-hood; that it has insisted on magic and mysteries, and has forced the priesthood to produce them. But then, how dreadful is the system that puts good men to such uses!

And although it is true that in its origin a priesthood is the effect of an evil already existing, a symptom of social disease rather than a cause of it, yet, once being created and made powerful, it tends in many ways to prolong and increase the disease which gave it birth. One of these ways is so marked and of such practical importance that we are bound to consider it here: I mean the education of children. If there is one lesson which history forces upon us in every page, it is this: *Keep your children away from the priest, or he will make them the enemies of mankind.* It is not the Catholic clergy and those like them who are alone to be dreaded in this matter; even the representatives of apparent-ly harmless religions may do incalculable mischief if they get education into their hands. To the early Muslims the mosque was the one public building in every place where public business could be transacted; and so it was naturally the place of primary education, which they held to be a matter of supreme importance. By and by, as the clergy grew up, the mosque was gradually usurped by them, and primary education fell into their hands. Then ensued a 'revival of religion;' religion became a fanaticism: books were burnt and universities were closed; the empire rotted away in East and West, until it was conquered by Turkish sav-ages in Asia and by Christian savages in Spain.

The labours of students of the early history of institutions—notably Sir Henry Maine and M. de Laveleye[69]—have disclosed to us an ele-ment of society which appears to have existed in all times and places,

---

67 ['Always everywhere and by everyone.']
68 [John Russell, Viscount Amberley (1842–76), was a British politician and writer. He held, for the time, unorthodox religious view and was supportive of birth control and votes for women. This contributed to the end of his short career as an MP.]
69 [Émile Louis Victor de Laveleye (1822–92) was a Belgian economist.]

and which is the basis of our own social structure. The village community, or commune, or township, found in tribes of the most varied race and time, has so modified itself as to get adapted in one place or another to all the different conditions of human existence. This union of men to work for a common object has transformed them from wild animals into tame ones. Century by century the educating process of the social life has been working at human nature; it has built itself into our inmost soul. Such as we are—moral and rational beings—thinking and talking in general conceptions about the facts that make up our life, feeling a necessity to act, not for ourselves, but for Ourself, for the larger life of Man in which we are elements; such moral and rational beings, I say, Man has made us. By Man I mean men organized into a society, which fights for its life, not only as a mere collection of men who must separately be kept alive, but as a society. It must fight not only against external enemies, but against treason and disruption within it. Hence comes the unity of interest of all its members; each of them has to feel that he is not himself only but a part of all the rest. Conscience—the sense of right and wrong—springs out of the habit of judging things from the point of view of all and not of one. It is Ourself, not ourselves, that makes for righteousness.

The codes of morality, then, which are adopted into various religions, and afterward taught as parts of religious systems, are derived from secular sources. The most ancient version of the Ten Commandments, whatever the investigations of scholars may make it out to be, originates, not in the thunders of Sinai, but in the peaceful life of men on the plains of Chaldaea.[70] Conscience is the voice of Man ingrained into our hearts, commanding us to work for Man.

Religions differ in the treatment which they give to this most sacred heirloom of our past history. Sometimes they invert its precepts—telling men to be submissive under oppression because the powers that be are ordained of God; telling them to believe where they have not seen, and to play with falsehood in order that a particular doctrine may prevail, instead of seeking for truth whatever it may be; telling them to betray their country for the sake of their church. But there is one great distinction to which I wish, in conclusion, to call special attention—a

---

70 [Chaldaea was a Semitic-speaking nation which existed between the late tenth or early ninth and mid-sixth centuries BC. It was located along the Euphrates River in what is now modern-day Iran, Iraq and Syria.]

distinction between two kinds of religious emotion which bear upon the conduct of men.

We said that conscience is the voice of Man within us, commanding us to work for Man. We do not know this immediately by our own experience; we only know that something within us commands us to work for Man. This fact men have tried to explain; and they have thought, for the most part, that this voice was the voice of a God. But the explanation takes two different forms: the God may speak in us for Man's sake, or for his own sake. If he speaks for his own sake—and this is what generally happens when he has priests who lay claim to a magical character and powers—our allegiance is apt to be taken away from Man, and transferred to the God. When we love our brother for the sake of our brother, we help all men to grow in the right; but when we love our brother for the sake of somebody else, who is very likely to damn our brother, it very soon comes to burning him alive for his soul's health. When men respect human life for the sake of Man, tranquillity, order and progress go hand in hand; but those who only respected human life because God had forbidden murder have set their mark upon Europe in fifteen centuries of blood and fire.

These are only two examples of a general rule. Wherever the allegiance of men has been diverted from Man to some divinity who speaks to men for his own sake and seeks his own glory, one thing has happened. The right precepts might be enforced, but they were enforced upon wrong grounds, and they were not obeyed. But right precepts are not always enforced; the fact that the fountains of morality have been poisoned makes it easy to substitute wrong precepts for right ones.

To this same treason against humanity belongs the claim of the priesthood to take away the guilt of a sinner after confession has been made to it. The Catholic priest professes to act as an ambassador for his God, and to absolve the guilty man by conveying to him the forgiveness of heaven. If his credentials were ever so sure, if he were indeed the ambassador of a superhuman power, the claim would be treasonable. Can the favour of the Tsar make guiltless the murderer of old men and women and children in Circassian valleys?[71] Can the pardon of the Sultan make clean the bloody hands of a Pasha? As little can any God forgive sins committed against man. When men think he can, they compound for old sins which the God did not like by committing new

---

71 [Circassia is a part of the north Caucasus and the shore of the Black Sea. Tsar Peter the Great conquered the area during the Russo-Circassian War (1763–1864).]

ones which he does like. Many a remorseful despot has atoned for the levities of his youth by the persecution of heretics in his old age. That frightful crime, the adulteration of food, could not possibly be so common among us if men were not taught to regard it as merely objectionable because it is remotely connected with stealing, of which God has expressed his disapproval in the Decalogue; and therefore as quite, naturally set right by a punctual attendance at church on Sundays. When a Ritualist breaks his fast before celebrating the Holy Communion, his deity can forgive him if he likes, for the matter concerns nobody else; but no deity can forgive him for preventing his parishioners from setting up a public library and reading-room for fear they should read Mr. Darwin's works in it. That sin is committed against the people, and a God cannot take it away.

I call those religions which undermine the supreme allegiance of the conscience to Man *ultramontane*[72] religions, because they seek their springs of action *ultra montes*,[73] outside of the common experience and daily life of man. And I remark about them that they are especially apt to teach wrong precepts, and that even when they command men to do the right things they put the command upon wrong motives, and do not get the things done.

But there are forms of religious emotion which do not thus undermine the conscience. Far be it from me to under-value the help and strength which many of the bravest of our brethren have drawn from the thought of an unseen helper of men. He who, wearied or stricken in the fight with the powers of darkness, asks himself in a solitary place, 'Is it all for nothing? shall we indeed be overthrown?'—he does find something which may justify that thought. In such a moment of utter sincerity, when a man has bared his own soul before the immensities and the eternities, a presence in which his own poor personality is shrivelled into nothingness arises within him, and says, as plainly as words can say, 'I am with thee, and I am greater than thou.' Many names of Gods, of many shapes, have men given to this presence; seeking by names and pictures to know more clearly and to remember more continually the guide and the helper of men. No such comradeship with the Great Companion shall have anything but reverence from

---

72 [This term is usually means advocating supreme papal authority in matters of faith and discipline.]

73 ['Beyond the.']

me, who have known the divine gentleness of Denison Maurice,[74] the strong and healthy practical instinct of Charles Kingsley,[75] and who now revere with all my heart the teaching of James Martineau.[76] They seem to me, one and all, to be reaching forward with loving anticipation to a clearer vision which is yet to come—*tendebantque manus ripae ulterioris amore.*[77] For, after all, such a helper of men, outside of humanity, the truth will not allow us to see. The dim and shadowy outlines of the superhuman deity fade slowly away from before us; and as the mist of his presence floats aside, we perceive with greater and greater clearness the shape of a yet grander and nobler figure—of Him who made all Gods and shall unmake them. From the dim dawn of history, and from the inmost depth of every soul, the face of our father Man looks out upon us with the fire of eternal youth in his eyes, and says, 'Before Jehovah was, I am!'

---

74 [John Frederick Denison Maurice (1805-72), was an English major theologian of the Church of England, a prolific author and one of the founders of Christian Socialism.]

75 [Charles Kingsley (1819-75) was an English priest of the Church of England, a university professor, social reformer, historian and novelist. He is particularly associated with Christian socialism, the working men's college, and forming labour cooperatives that failed but led to the working reforms of the progressive era.]

76 [James Martineau (1805-1900) was an English religious philosopher.]

77 ['They reached out their hands longing for the further shore.' A partial quote from *The Aeneid* by Virgil, the ancient Roman poet.]

www.ingramcontent.com/pod-product-compliance
Lightning Source LLC
LaVergne TN
LVHW021130080426
835511LV00010B/1807

* 9 7 8 1 9 1 0 1 4 6 3 1 6 *